Creating Accepting Communities

Report of the Mind Inquiry into social
exclusion and mental health problems

Inquiry panel
Lincoln Crawford
David Crepaz-Keay
Ivan Massow
Julia Neuberger
Denise Platt
Pola Manzila Uddin

Report author
Sara Dunn

Mind works on behalf of all those who experience mental distress, campaigning for their right to lead an active and valued life in the community. Mind established this Inquiry as part of its three-year 'Respect' campaign, aimed at highlighting the discrimination in all areas of life experienced by those who have mental health problems.

First published November 1999 by
Mind Publications
15–19 Broadway
London E15 4BQ
Tel. 020 8221 9666
Fax. 020 8534 6399
e.mail. publications@mind.org.uk

ISBN 1 874690 87 1

Written by Sara Dunn
Designed by Adkins Design
Printed by Fretwells Ltd
Cover image by Daniel Pudles

CONTENTS

ACKNOWLEDGEMENTS

Many people have worked tirelessly to make this Inquiry happen.

The Mind Inquiry Secretariat – Mary Ellen Coyte (Mind Inquiry co-ordinator), Sara Dunn (Mind Inquiry report author and editor), Christine Sheppard (Mind Inquiry co-ordinator) and Patrick Vernon (regional director, South East Mind and *Creating Accepting Communities* project director) – would like to thank: the members of the Inquiry Panel – Lincoln Crawford, David Crepaz-Keay, Ivan Massow, Julia Neuberger, Denise Platt and Pola Manzila Uddin; all those who submitted oral and written evidence (including those who wish to remain anonymous and are not included in the appendices); Grace Aghoghovbia (regional administrator, South East Mind); Pauline Allan (office services, Mind); Gina Amankwah (administrative assistant, South East Mind); Sue Baker (head of media relations, Mind); Peter Bates (National Development Team); Jabeer Butt (consultant, REU); Anny Brackx (director of corporate promotion, Mind); Ian Bynoe (formerly chief solicitor, Mind); Alison Cobb (policy officer, Mind); Sophie Corlett (policy director, SKILL); Angela Hendra (communications manager, Mind); Fiona Jackson (press officer, Mind); Angela McHarron (regional officer, West Midlands Mind); Gerry McNamara (office services, Mind); Margaret Pedler (head of policy and parliamentary unit, Mind); David Piper (office services, Mind); Liz Sayce (formerly policy director, Mind); Claire Williams (policy information officer, Mind Cymru); George Stewart (information officer, Mind); Jenny Willmot (policy officer, Mind); Melba Wilson (policy director, Mind).

The Panel members would like to thank the Mind Inquiry Secretariat, and all those who submitted oral and written evidence, whose contributions made this report.

Mind is very grateful to the Department of Health for the funding of this Inquiry. Many thanks also to the Corporation of London and to the King's Fund for the use of their premises for the Panel sessions.

FOREWORD

The most fascinating aspect of this Inquiry has been hearing about solutions to problems when I didn't previously know the problems even existed. Before the Inquiry, I had some personal experience of the consequences of mental illness. I knew something of the consequences of discrimination and prejudice of different types, but I hadn't given much thought to day-to-day living with mental ill-health.

Over the twelve months of the Inquiry that changed. We heard of discrimination against people with mental health problems in service provision, in education, in employment – in every aspect of life. The most powerful evidence came from people who had received psychiatric diagnoses. These people were doctors, health service workers, managers, office workers and teachers. They came from a wide range of social backgrounds. They had little in common except that as soon as they received their diagnosis, their world changed. Not because of their condition but because they had suddenly been marked *different*. They had become *mad* people.

I was surprised by the number of ways society excludes people. People lost business interests because of company law, they lost access to financial services, courts denied them access to their children. As if to rub salt into the wound, social exclusion resulting from psychiatric diagnosis is even excluded from the Government's own Social Exclusion Unit.

But amongst the despair lies hope. We saw beacons of good practice, we saw people taking personal risks to challenge discrimination. Above all, we saw people *surviving*, and returning to fight again. Chairing this Inquiry has been a humbling experience, and I am honoured to have been asked.

This report does not make easy reading, but anyone who is serious about mental health issues, or worried about what would happen to them if they ever went into crisis, should read this and want to change things.

Ivan Massow
Chair of the *Creating Accepting Communities Inquiry*

Social inclusion must come down to somewhere to live, something to do, someone to love. It's as simple – and as complicated – as that. There are all kinds of barriers to people with mental health problems having those three things. *Charles Fraser, Inquiry witness*

When I told my boss I was being taken into hospital his reaction said it all. He sat back in his seat wanting to keep as far away from me as possible. As soon as mental illness is mentioned people literally back off from you. *Jo, Inquiry witness*

Putting 'types' of people together and pretending an alternative and equally valid community has been formed does not work. They just get to be meaningless together. *Micheline Mason, Inquiry witness*

Mental health services need a new vision. We need to focus on inclusion, not exclusion, on building communities, rather than looking for problems; we need to focus on friendships rather than homicides. *Peter Bates, Inquiry witness*

The aims of the Mind Inquiry

- to find out the extent and the nature of the social exclusion experienced by people with mental health problems in Britain today

- to listen directly to the views of mental health service users on their experience of exclusion and the ways to combat it

- to hear directly from those working in mental health services how they feel social exclusion can best be tackled

- to find out from general employers, and providers of goods and services, what help they need to counter the exclusion of people with mental health problems from mainstream society.

10 guiding principles for social inclusion

- A healthy society is one that maximises opportunity for each of its members, regardless of their circumstances.

- A healthy society is also one that embraces diversity and is not threatened by cultures, beliefs or behaviours outside society's norms.

- Nobody is a 'burden' on society. Everyone is part of society and has an inherent and absolute worth as a human being.

- Promoting social inclusion involves the active fostering of the mutual inter-dependence between individuals, groups of people and the state.

- The social exclusion of any group of people creates schisms that are bad not only for the mental health of excluded individuals but for the mental health of society as a whole.

- Social excusion is a 'compound' process. Its interconnections mean exclusion in one area of life often leads to exclusion in another.

- Inclusion therefore needs to be addressed in a holistic way. The catalysts that promote inclusion will have wide-ranging benefits, for individuals and communities.

- Specialist services must be conceived as stepping-stones to inclusion, not departure-points for exclusion. The ultimate aim of inclusion is enabling participation in the mainstream of society for all those who desire it.

- Excluded groups are experts by experience. All processes of consultation, policy-making and practice must not just include, but be driven by, the views and needs of excluded groups.

- Promoting inclusion means leading public opinion. Clear and consistent messages from Government, public bodies and the voluntary sector are the only way to tackle 'them and us' thinking.

Inquiry evidence

The experience of exclusion

Work

> We retrain people with mental health problems to get them back into employment. We have good contacts in business and industry, but we haven't been able to place people at all easily. There is still so much fear. *Simon Morris, Inquiry witness*

- There are many openly discriminatory practices in workplaces with regard to mental ill-health.
- Service users have a justified fear of discrimination at work, which prevents disclosure of past or current ill-health and discourages people from applying for jobs in the first place.
- Employers feel under-prepared and under-informed in dealing with mental health issues.
- Mental health services, in both clinical and support settings, do not see promoting work for service users as part of their role.

Education and training

> The entire education system is underpinned by an unaware but deeply entrenched policy of segregation based on totally false concepts of 'ability' and 'disability'. *Micheline Mason, Inquiry witness*

- There is little knowledge or understanding of mental health issues in many schools, colleges or universities.
- Educational bodies do not know where to go for guidance, due in part to the lack of a central body promoting access to education for people with mental health problems.
- Practical support mechanisms for people with mental health problems – for example benefits advice, transport, on-campus support – are almost non-existent within further and higher education.
- The structure of many courses – for example limited time-frames for completion – can discriminate against people with mental health problems.

Daily living

> It is easier to live in society with a prison record than a psychiatric record. *Hywel Davies, Inquiry witness*

- Many users feel that a psychiatric diagnosis makes them non-citizens, with no rights, no credibility and no redress.
- The ostracisation of mental health service users leads to difficulties in establishing social networks, a lack of informal job contacts, and a lack of access to everyday goods and services.
- People from minority ethnic groups who experience mental health problems are more than doubly excluded. Racist discrimination has a material impact on mental health. Gender stereotyping can also have detrimental impacts on both men and women with mental health problems.
- Families and carers can be affected by the discrimination experienced by people with mental health problems, leading to ruptured support networks and the exclusion of carers by the wider community.
- The media has tremendous power in creating and perpetuating discriminatory attitudes towards people with a mental illness diagnosis.

Mental health services

> The fundamental point is that discrimination arises because of the diagnosis, not as a result of the condition itself. *Simon Foster, Inquiry witness*

- Mental health services focus on the clinical to the detriment of the social. Professionals must understand mental health problems in relation to the disabling effects of discrimination.
- This lack of understanding impacts particularly on users from minority groups, such as minority ethnic groups, women, lesbians and gay men, or people with physical or sensory impairments.
- Instead of leading to a therapeutic or supportive process, a psychiatric diagnosis can be the start of social exclusion. This process is triggered in part by the nature of psychiatric services themselves, which can be experienced as ghettoised and stigmatising.
- The NHS engages in excluding and discriminatory behaviour towards people with mental health problems, who may find themselves struck off GP lists, or receiving inadequate secondary or tertiary general health care.

Promoting inclusion

Work

> We promote rehabilitation and support for staff during and after illness, including mental health problems. We understand and subscribe to the suggestions for best practice with regard to mental health, and are open to guidance on how best to translate these into action. *Norwich Union (written evidence)*

- Many employers are starting to recognise that creating mentally healthy workplaces, including supporting workers who experience or have previously experienced mental ill-health, constitutes good employment practice.
- Benefit reform, as outlined in the Inquiry recommendations, can go a long way toward removing barriers to employment for mental health service users.
- Very often, reasonable adjustments in relation to mental health (as required by the Disability Discrimination Act) are positive all round. All employees have mental health needs, and measures to support people with particular problems will benefit all.
- There are some pioneering, successful models of good employment practice within the NHS itself, which can be disseminated and built upon.

Education and training

> If you set up a class in an ordinary college for mental health service users only, it's a good start. But it's only a stepping-stone. Mainstream registration alongside ordinary citizens is more like inclusion in my book. *Peter Bates, Inquiry witness*

- Some institutions have established starter courses for people with mental health problems, geared to students' needs. These are vital stepping-stones on the way to full inclusion, i.e. enrolment in mainstream education for those who want it.
- Lessons for promoting mentally healthy schools come from the disability movement's campaigns for inclusive schools. Models of giving back control to service users – in this case children – do exist, and they can make a huge contribution to children's mental health.

- Some effective mental health promotion and mental illness prevention does happen on-campus. The forging of links between health and social services and education bodies can facilitate the opening up of access to education for existing mental health service users.

Arts and media

> The arts can play a major role in developing excluded groups' confidence and ability to take an active role in their communities.
> *Theatre in Prisons and Probation Centres (written evidence)*

- It is increasingly recognised that the arts can play a catalytic role in promoting social inclusion, both through the participative processes involved and the innovative 'products' created.
- Just as media images have been a force for exclusion, they can be a force for inclusion. Mental health services and service users are becoming strategic in accessing and using the media.
- Promoting positive role models – famous people and 'ordinary' people talking about living with mental ill-health – has a tremendous power to demystify and destigmatise.
- Media monitoring has an increasingly positive role to play. Media organisations are sensitive to their public's views, and coordinated action to get service users' views onto producers' agendas has tangible results.

Daily living

> What we have found is that we are actually surrounded by allies in the move for inclusion. We found experts in inclusion just around the corner, disguised as teachers, as parents of children with disabilities, as shopkeepers. We found that if we asked people to open up, to include others, then often they would say 'Yes'. *Peter Bates, Inquiry witness*

- There are inspiring examples where health and social services are going out into the community, talking to people – pub landlords, gym managers, shopkeepers – and building bridges so that mental health service users can be included back into their local communities.
- Imaginative schemes such as LETS (local exchange trading schemes) have transformed the lives of some mental health service users. The promotion

of social firms, LETS schemes and other innovative forms of creating value and exchanging goods is slowly moving up the agenda of both social services and some local authorities.

- Anti-discrimination legislation has a potentially large role to play in ensuring that providers of goods and services – shops, banks, financial services, leisure services and so on – do not discriminate against people with mental health problems. The new Disability Rights Commission can take a pro-active role in backing up legal provision.

Mental health services

> A programme of community dialogue and education must be at the centre of any mental health strategy. *Community Housing and Therapy (written evidence)*

- A new focus on social inclusion is encouraging mental health services to look beyond their traditional clinical boundaries and to address the processes of discrimination and exclusion.
- Community development activities and partnerships that stretch beyond health and social services are beginning to gain momentum. Health Action Zones, Healthy Living Centres, Sure Start and other Government initiatives, as well as the policies outlined in the recent public health white paper *Saving Lives: Our Healthier Nation,* are all contributing to a more holistic view of mental health and illness.
- Mental health services are beginning to see employment as a key factor in creating and maintaining mental health. Mental health trusts are seeking collaboration with employment agencies and other local bodies to promote employment for service users.
- Some mental health trusts are forging the way ahead by instituting positive and inclusive employment practice within their own workforces.

The Inquiry's recommendations

- The social exclusion of people with mental health problems needs to be tackled at national policy level. The Government's Social Exclusion Unit, whose cross-departmental remit makes it ideally placed, should urgently review all Government policy as it affects those with mental health problems.

- Comprehensive and enforceable anti-discrimination legislation, based on an inclusive definition of disability, must replace the current limited Disability Discrimination Act. The new Disability Rights Commission must take a pro-active approach to the enforcement of any new anti-discrimination law.

- The Government's proposed new Mental Health Act should enshrine the principle of non-discrimination on grounds of mental ill-health.

- Further benefit reforms to 'make work pay' and overcome the many barriers to employment for people with mental health problems must be implemented.

- The Government and national health education and promotion agencies, in partnership with local authorities, voluntary bodies and mental health service providers, should use the public education resources at their disposal to challenge the perception of the link between violence and mental ill-health.

- A coordinated national initiative must be established to promote employment for mental health service users across the country.

- Mental health services must ensure that the experience of exclusion is included in all aspects of service assessments such as the Care Programme Approach. Improvements outlined in the National Service Framework for Mental Health are meaningless if clinical mental health issues are divorced from the everyday reality of people's lives.

- Mental health services must work in partnership with service users with the aim of ensuring that they have access to activities and relationships in the communities of their choice, and can, as far as possible, live the lives that they choose.

- Mental health service providers in both the statutory and voluntary sectors need to take the lead as employers, by valuing the contribution users bring to mental health work and by encouraging their appointment.

- Local authorities, education bodies, employment agencies and all health and social services providers have a role, and a stake, in promoting social inclusion for people with mental health problems. Mental health services themselves must take a lead in initiating links with agencies outside their traditional working partners. Effective working together can begin to create a more inclusive and a mentally healthier society.

The Mind Inquiry:

when, why and what

The advent of the New Labour Government in May 1997, with its new emphasis on the interrelated nature of so many social problems, opened up a new opportunity for looking at the interactions between different forms of deprivation and discrimination. One of the first concrete results of this new approach was the creation of the Government's Social Exclusion Unit (SEU) (see Glossary).

According to the SEU, social exclusion 'is a shorthand label for what can happen when individuals or areas suffer from a combination of linked problems such as unemployment, poor skills, low incomes, poor housing, high crime environments, bad health and family breakdown' (SEU 1999). While there are existing Government policies aimed at tackling these individually, the SEU points out that hitherto 'Government programmes have been less good at tackling the interactions between these problems and at preventing them arising in the first place' (SEU 1999).

The Government's new emphasis on joined-up approaches to problems, in looking at a number of different but clearly interrelated issues simultaneously, was greatly welcomed by many in the mental health field.

In 1996 Mind (the National Association for Mental Health) began its three-year 'Respect' Campaign, aimed at highlighting and combating the discrimination in all walks of life experienced by people with mental health problems. In autumn 1997, Mind saw the need to generate specific mental health input into the increasing amount of research, policy and practice gathering momentum under the banner of social exclusion.

Mind was very keen that any discussion of mental health and social exclusion should take as its starting point the everyday experience of those involved. This meant listening directly to the opinions and experiences of

. . . .

people who have been or are being excluded from society as a result of being diagnosed with mental ill-health. It also meant listening to those who are working to reduce that exclusion, in the voluntary, statutory and commercial sectors.

Mind felt it important to gather together an independent Panel, comprising people with expertise in a range of areas of voluntary, statutory, commercial and public life. The Panel has used that expertise to synthesise the evidence into a compelling portrait not only of what exclusion is, and why it might happen, but also what can be done to tackle it. Mind is deeply grateful to the Chair Ivan Massow and to all members of the Panel for their commitment and invaluable work on this Inquiry.

The process of collecting evidence was begun in the spring of 1998. Calls for evidence were placed in national mental health publications, and leaflets distributed to more than 7,000 named individuals and organisations throughout Mind's extensive networks. (These include MindLink [mental health service user network], Diverse Minds [black and minority ethnic mental health network], *OpenMind* [bi-monthly subscription journal], and local Mind Associations [220 service-providing organisations nationally]). Mind also solicited evidence from key individuals and organisations.

The Inquiry Secretariat received responses (detailed in Appendices c and d) from hundreds of individuals, groups and organisations, ranging from high street retailers to individual users, NHS trusts to small voluntary groups.[1] The organisations that responded covered a very broad sweep of the statutory and voluntary sectors, including the police, the Church of England, black, Asian, Jewish, Muslim and Irish organisations, gay and lesbian groups and homelessness organisations. Mental health specific bodies included both statutory and voluntary groups, ranging widely in size, focus and geographical location. The bulk of the evidence received was from individuals or groups in the south east of England, although there were submissions from right across Great Britain and also from Ireland.

Businesses that responded to the initial questionnaire included retail chains, high street banks, building societies, insurance companies and service utilities. Very few of them had examples of good practice relating to people with mental health problems, but all of them regarded this as an omission they would like to address. Many businesses said they needed advice and training about tackling mental health issues.

---

1 *A number of respondents requested complete anonymity, and are not therefore included in the Appendices. All evidence was of great value to the Inquiry, and informed the Panel's conclusions and recommendations.*

The range and quality of evidence received was testimony both to the extent to which users of mental health services are excluded, and the passionate commitment of many people to challenge that exclusion. Mind and the Panel are very grateful to all those who took the time to respond. The preliminary findings threw up examples of the exclusion of people with mental health problems in every sphere of public and private life. Examples ranged from difficulties in getting a driving licence or booking a holiday, to discriminatory attitudes from insurance companies, through to barriers blocking access to health care or employment.

The Inquiry Secretariat selected 40 witnesses who best represented the range of themes and opinions received in the written evidence to give oral evidence to the Panel, and to respond to the Panel's questions. This report contains much of the oral evidence the Panel heard, as well as selections from the written evidence.[2]

While the Inquiry covered a great deal of productive ground, the evidence and recommendations cannot cover all aspects of this vast and extremely complex area. There are several areas in which the Panel felt there was a pressing need for further investigation. In particular, the exclusion of older people with mental health problems urgently needs to be addressed. The Panel noted that the current Government's emphasis on improving access to training, education and jobs as the key to reducing social exclusion will be of little use to the huge majority of older people with mental health problems. The Panel also noted the need for further research and development work in the area of housing policy and practice, and its impact on issues of mental ill-health and social exclusion.

The Mind Inquiry: where next

The Inquiry has been a galvanising process for all concerned. The Panel and Mind hope that the publication and dissemination of this report will spur others on in the drive towards fair, effective and progressive mental health care for everyone. The report's findings make it clear that mental health care is an issue for everyone who is concerned about quality of life for our communities, not just those in the mental health field. And also that those within the mental health field need to look beyond their traditional clinical

---

2 It should be noted that the premise of the Inquiry was that oral witnesses were appearing in a personal capacity. While the organisations for which oral witnesses worked at the time of giving evidence have been indicated, witnesses' views should not necessarily be taken as the views of their particular organisation.

and social care boundaries if they are to make genuine moves towards promoting social inclusion for users.

The evidence gathered by this Inquiry confirms without equivocation that people with mental health problems are seriously excluded in British society today. This exclusion arises not from the mental health problems themselves, but from the assumptions and prejudices that are attached to the diagnosis – by members of the local community, and also by health and social care professionals.

As is detailed in Chapter 4, the Panel strongly recommends that the Government's Social Exclusion Unit (SEU), which hitherto has 'excluded' mental health issues, should urgently review Government policy in this area. The National Service Framework for Mental Health (see Glossary) contains much that is warmly welcomed by those seeking to help people who experience mental health problems. But the National Service Framework cannot function in isolation from how service users are treated 'in the community'. Many of the recommendations addressed to Government in Chapter 4 are aimed at Departments other than the Department of Health. It is imperative therefore that the social exclusion of those with mental health problems is not only recognised, but addressed by a senior, cross-Government unit. The Panel feels that the SEU is ideally placed to take forward this work.

Mind itself will use this report as one of the foundations on which to build its own social inclusion agenda. The main thrust of Mind's work will be the development of a model for promoting quality of life for people with mental health problems. The intention is to create a flexible model that will be usable by local authorities and education and employment bodies as well as public health and mental health services. The model, which will incorporate clinical and non-clinical outcomes, will develop measures in the areas of discrimination prevention, effective partnerships, physical and mental health improvement, and enabling fair access to opportunities. Specific foci will be race and culture, the arts and sport, employment, and neighbourhood inclusion.

Mind will develop the model in collaboration with a number of other voluntary and statutory bodies, and aims to pilot the measures in two test areas in the community within two years.

A note on language

Language is often a vexed topic in mental health. In this report we have used the terms 'mental health problems' and 'mental ill-health' interchangeably. All witnesses' evidence is quoted verbatim. The Panel as a whole was less interested in questions of semantics than in allowing people to define their own experience and suggest their own solutions to problems.

The Panel took as a given that mental health problems can and should be defined as a 'disability' within the terms of the Disability Discrimination Act (see Glossary). The Panel also noted that alliances between mental health groups and other disability organisations were greatly to be welcomed, since both mental health service users and those with physical or sensory impairments had much to gain by united action.

CHAPTER 1

'Outside looking in':

the social exclusion of people with mental health problems

1.1 Existing research

There is mounting evidence of the discrimination experienced by people with mental health problems in Britain. This discrimination results in their systematic exclusion from society. Social exclusion operates in all areas of life – daily living, work and training, and access to services, including health, financial, consumer and leisure services.

Community care policies of recent decades have changed the location of health and social services for people with mental health problems. But the ethos of segregation that underpinned mass institutionalisation remains. The brick walls of the old institutions have been replaced by economic and social barriers within 'the community'; they are less obvious, but just as effective.

Many users and ex-users of psychiatric services feel that discriminatory attitudes have been made worse in recent years by sensationalist media coverage of violent crimes committed by people with mental health problems. Such reporting misleadingly and damagingly links mental ill-health with a propensity to violence. This link then provides spurious justification for pushing people with mental health problems to the very margins of society.

Employment

Research repeatedly shows that people with disabilities are significantly more excluded from the labour market than any other group. Unemployment is two-and-a-half times as high and economic inactivity twice as high amongst disabled people as among non-disabled. Within this group, people with mental health problems have much higher rates of economic inactivity than those with physical or sensory impairments (Howarth *et al.* 1998). The Office for National Statistics (ONS) (1998) reported that only 17 per cent of working-age people with a diagnosis of serious mental ill-health are economically active.

Research in the United States (Baron *et al.* 1996) has found that 70 per cent of people diagnosed with a serious mental illness identify work as a key life-goal. British surveys reveal that long-term users of mental health day-services retain their ambition to work, despite scant support to achieve it (Bates 1996).

Read and Baker (1996), reported that 34 per cent of 778 users of mental health services surveyed reported being dismissed or forced to resign from their jobs. Of these, 20 per cent worked in the 'caring professions' – as nurses, social workers or other NHS employees. Thirty-nine per cent of respondents felt they had been denied a job because of their diagnosis; and 52 per cent had concealed their psychiatric history for fear of losing their job. A massive 69 per cent of users in this survey had been deterred from even applying for work because of their fear of being unfairly treated. Other recent surveys show very similar findings: Link *et al.* (1997) found that 75 per cent of people with a serious mental illness diagnosis would not tell a prospective employer; Patrick (1994) reported that 29 per cent of service users questioned had been refused employment for failing a medical, and 26 per cent had been dismissed or refused promotion because of mental health problems. Many respondents in these surveys commented that they would not even apply for jobs because they knew they would not get them (Patrick 1994).

Service users' fears are well justified. Glozier (1998) tested the attitudes of major UK companies to mental health problems of potential employees. Two hundred personnel managers were asked to assess employment prospects based on two vignettes of job applicants who had recovered from a health problem, identical except for the diagnosis of either diabetes or depression. The applicant with depression had significantly reduced chances of employment. Such findings are echoed by earlier evidence: Manning and White (1995) found systematic discrimination by employers against those who have or have had a mental health problem, and Sinclair's earlier study (1986) showed similar patterns of discriminatory attitudes by employers towards those who 'confessed' to mental ill-health.

And the pattern is a circular one; long-term unemployment has considerable negative effects on health, including mental health. People experiencing long-term unemployment have heightened risks of developing depression and of committing suicide (Howarth *et al.* 1998). According to the Government's White Paper *Saving Lives: Our Healthier Nation* (DoH 1999) unemployed people are twice as likely to suffer from depression as people in work.

Daily living: access to goods, services and social networks
One survey (Read and Baker 1996) found that 47 per cent of 778 mental health service users surveyed had been verbally or physically abused in public – for instance had eggs thrown at them while being called 'nutter', or had dog faeces or lighted paper put through their letter box.

A literature search by Repper and Brooker (1996) found that a general post-war trend of increasing tolerance towards people with mental illness went into reverse in the early 1990s, with public fears beginning to increase. Fifty per cent of Read and Baker's (1996) respondents felt they had been unfairly treated in the general (non-psychiatric) health system. Comments included: 'Every genuine physical illness I have had over the last twenty years has first been dismissed as anxiety, depression or stress'; 'I moved house when I was eight months pregnant, and my midwife wrote "hypomanic" in large red letters across my notes. No GP in my new area would take me on.'

Insurance was another very problematic area: 'I have not even tried to get insurance, as my insurers in the past had put additional costs onto policies because of my background.' Twenty-five per cent of users had been turned down by a finance or insurance company (Read and Baker 1996).

Contrary to media portrayals (see below) people with mental health problems are more likely to be *victims* of violence than the perpetrators (Murphy 1991). The justice system often does not protect victims with mental health problems, as they are often considered unreliable witnesses (Pedler 1998; Home Office 1998).

Research on the experiences of black and minority ethnic users of mental health services reveals doubly prejudiced attitudes about race and mental health problems on the part of the public (Wilson and Francis 1997; Fernando *et al.* 1998).

Violence and the media
There is an unquestioning acceptance in the media of the 'rising toll of killings' as a result of community care. This is in defiance of the facts. Taylor and Gunn (1999) reviewed Home Office criminal statistics for England and Wales between 1957 and 1995, and found little fluctuation in the numbers of people with a mental illness diagnosis committing criminal homicide

over the 38-year period, and a 3 per cent annual decline in their contribution to the official statistics. The UK Audit Commission's figures (1994) for the last 20 years showed no increase in homicides by people with mental health problems, a period in which homicides generally had doubled.

Preliminary findings of the most comprehensive research ever undertaken in this area, the MacArthur Violence Risk Assessment Study in the United States (MacArthur Foundation 1999), suggest that violence is linked to substance (illicit drug and alcohol) misuse, and that mental disorder is linked only insofar as it is associated with substance misuse. This echoes other international research in the area, including a recent Australian study (Mullen *et al.* 1998), which found that people diagnosed with schizophrenia were significantly less likely to commit a violent offence than alcohol or drug users who did not have a mental illness diagnosis.

Despite all of this evidence, research by Philo (1996) found that two-thirds of news and current affairs coverage made a link between mental ill-health and violence. Many users feel that media reporting influences greatly how other people perceive them. Media myths were found to be so potent that they even overrode people's lived experiences. People with mental health problems themselves reported feeling 'like monsters', because that's how they were portrayed on TV. People who lived near mental health facilities said they were worried that patients would be violent – even though their actual experience was to the contrary – because 'that's the way things come across on TV and films' (Philo 1996).

Attention has also been drawn to the racist nature of much mental health reporting. Fernando *et al.* (1998) point out in particular that African-Caribbean men who may have mental health problems and who also commit a violent crime are tried, convicted and sentenced in the press. Lurid conflations of stereotypes of blackness, madness and dangerousness mean that rare violent incidents receive coverage out of all proportion to their prevalence.

Mental health services

Repper *et al.* (1997) revealed the frequency and level of nimby ('not in my back yard') opposition to community mental health facilities, both residential and drop in. Over two-thirds of statutory and voluntary mental health service providers had experienced nimby campaigns. Community opposition ranged from protest letters and meetings and legal action, to graffiti, verbal abuse and violence. Most services had to delay opening at least one facility because of nimbyism.

Assaults against people – particularly women – in institutions, by other patients or by staff, may be particularly under-reported, as the service users are vulnerable to retribution if they make a complaint (Sayce 1992; Pedler 1998). A recent survey of inpatient facilities reported that a third of patients did not feel personally secure, 71 per cent did not have a locker with a key, 55 per cent did not have a single room, and 20 per cent felt that washing facilities were not private enough (Moore and Gawith 1998).

Certain groups of mental health service users are particularly vulnerable. Research on the experiences of black users of mental health services reveals high levels of racism within mental health services (Wilson and Francis 1997; Fernando *et al.* 1998), with African-Caribbean men more likely to be compulsorily detained and less likely to be offered alternatives to drug treatment or electroconvulsive therapy (see Glossary).

Studies also show that older people are less likely to be referred for counselling than younger people (Mind 1997). Older people are also more likely to experience certain forms of mental ill-health – a greater proportion of 60 to 69 year olds have anxiety and depression than any other age group (Kind *et al.* 1998). Suicide rates for both sexes increase with age, with those at greatest risk over 74 years of age (Howarth *et al.* 1998).

The effect of exclusion on mental health

Research repeatedly shows that stressors such as poverty, unemployment, isolation and poor housing are in themselves triggers for mental ill-health (Howarth *et al.* 1998). A recent King's Fund report (Hoggett *et al.* 1999) showed clearly the links between mental ill-health and unemployment, living alone, insecure housing and low income. The groups most likely to experience these problems include people from minority ethnic groups, refugees, and single parents (especially mothers). In addition, people with mental health problems have high rates of coronary heart disease and other physical illnesses; standardised mortality rates for people diagnosed with schizophrenia are two-and-half times the average (DoH 1994). Office of Population and Census Surveys studies of mental health service users in institutions (including supported housing, hostels and so on) found that a quarter of people diagnosed with schizophrenia had a physical complaint, for example musculoskeletal, heart, circulatory and digestive problems (ONS 1996).

Once people have mental health problems, access to money, employment, social networks and secure housing becomes harder. As a consequence, many of the most vulnerable people in Britain today are caught in a spiral of social exclusion that is almost impossible to break.

1.2 **Evidence presented to the Inquiry**

The Inquiry Panel heard many witnesses testify to the process of exclusion experienced by mental health service users. Common themes were the disempowering and self-perpetuating nature of psychiatric diagnoses and labels, the prejudiced attitudes of others flowing from these labels, and an over-emphasis on the medical rather than the social causes – and consequences – of mental health problems.

Employment
The current Government places great emphasis on lack of access to work being one of the key causes of social exclusion. For users of mental health services, the obstacles to work are manifold.

Underlying many of the obstacles are employers' and colleagues' assumptions about what having been given a particular psychiatric diagnosis means. One witness described her experience of her employer discovering her mental health problems:

> I was working in a solicitor's as a trainee receptionist. I couldn't tell my boss I had to see a psychiatrist every week, so I told him I was on a training scheme one day a week. When I had to tell him I was being taken into hospital his reaction said it all. He sat back in his seat wanting to keep as far away from me as possible. As soon as mental illness is mentioned people literally back off from you. *Jo, mental health service user*

Another witness felt that her colleagues in the health service had, on occasion, displayed similar views:

> I've encountered all those hushed conversations along the lines of 'Is she really all right? Is she really able to work?' In my own place of work they have disappeared completely, but I still experience them elsewhere in my working life, particularly from other clinical psychologists, who have difficulties with a high-profile member of their own profession being open about having mental health problems. *Rachel Perkins, South West London and St George's Mental Health NHS Trust*

A GP who gave evidence to the Inquiry met with similar assumptions within the medical profession after he was diagnosed with manic depression by a fellow doctor in his practice:

> The problem starts once you go through the gates of a psychiatric hospital. Once you're labelled, the notes start building up. Psychiatrists won't retract anything, change the diagnosis, amend the notes. If you disagree with them, they say you lack insight. I was sectioned, and then I was sacked, because it was written into my general practice agreement that if a colleague is sectioned under the Mental Health Act [see Glossary] they can be removed from the practice. *Tom O'Brien, general practitioner*

The medical profession, while no better than other places of work, is no worse. Witnesses involved in trying to create and promote employment opportunities for service users spoke of great obstacles:

> We have an employment project trying to retrain people to get them back into employment. We have quite good contacts in business and industry, but we haven't been able to place people at all easily. There is still so much fear. *Simon Morris, Jewish Care*

> Black and minority ethnic people with mental health problems are very much excluded from employment opportunities. People are very isolated, they don't have social networks and often do not access social services either. So they do not get to know of employment opportunities, and if they do, they will often lack the confidence to try for them. *Marilyn Bryan, Awetu Black Mental Health Project*

Another witness drew attention to the Labour Force Survey figures for the working-age population with mental health problems, and the lack of a specific body promoting employment for service users:

> It is estimated that 12 per cent of people with mental health problems are in work, 4 per cent are looking for work and 84 per cent are not actually looking for work. If you compare this with other people with disabilities it is the largest or second largest group who are not actively looking for work. One of the things

employers say the whole time is 'We don't get disabled people applying.' Only 4 per cent of people with mental health problems are actually knocking on employers' doors.

I think this may be an explanation for why the mental health system is not focused on employment as an issue. There is no obvious lead voice on employment for people with mental health problems in this country. *Caroline Gooding, Employers' Forum on Disability*

This point was echoed by other witnesses:

An enormous number of CPNs and key workers have no experience of how to support people in work. So, very rarely is work part of people's care plans, very rarely do people consider going round and chatting up an employer to find a client a job. We need to change the focus of what we do as community long-term support to include this. *Rachel Perkins, South West London and St George's Mental Health NHS Trust*

Leading on from this, however, several witnesses felt strongly that people with mental health problems must not be 'set up to fail', that they must not be forced into work if it is not appropriate for them, and must be given the right support when they are there:

I'd probably be able to work if I had support for 4 days a week quite happily. But I have no support, nobody to talk things over with. I've already tried to go into work too quickly, had no support, and then gone into a severe depression. Then I had to go through the whole benefits process again. There is actually no point in applying for full-time work. I have to wait until I am 100 per cent well. *Jo, mental health service user*

I think the reason a lot of employment projects don't work is that they set people up to fail. People are so keen to get into full-time work, but I think this is a mistake. I would want people to start part-time and build up. People have a net potential but they have to release it at different levels over different periods of time. *Marilyn Bryan, Awetu Black Mental Health Project*

All the witnesses agreed on the issue of mainstreaming, of supporting people with mental health problems in the mainstream world of work:

Many people diagnosed with schizophrenia attend sheltered work facilities. These entail a number of disadvantages. The contract work usually available is boring and repetitive and pays very little. Clients are not brought into contact with ordinary members of the public. Hence the social relationships established are exclusively with providers and users of the psychiatric services. *Julian Leff, Institute of Psychiatry*

Some witnesses also raised a more fundamental question over the ways in which work is valued in society:

This society has a central notion about 'making an economic contribution'. This means that it is not enough to bring yourself, so that is a devaluation of the person. It also means you can only take rather than give for a limited period of time. So the person who has little to offer in economic terms becomes excluded. *Arthur Hawes, Archdeacon of Lincoln*

The right to be valued because we are alive, not just for our economic productiveness, is something disabled people and others in the inclusion movement are fighting for. This is to the benefit of everyone in society. *Micheline Mason, Alliance for Inclusive Education*

A related point was raised with regard to welfare to work legislation and its effects on young people with mental health problems:

I'm sceptical about how that works. An awful lot of thinking and resources are going into work and training initiatives for young people. Now for many young people this may be a very good thing. But for young people whose struggles are elsewhere at this point in time, and who require straightforward mental health support services, it is not helpful. Young people using our services feel great pressure, simply to continue getting benefits, to be part of welfare to work.

We know of a very sad story of a hostel where young people were quite aware that in order to avoid the difficulties of welfare to work legislation they would need their doctors to sign them off as sick. So there was a flurry of self-harming activity. This seemed so very unhelpful and inappropriate. It is important to value what Welfare to Work can bring into young people's lives, but also to recognise what it can't. *Alistair Cox, 42nd Street*

The issue of the benefits system as a huge barrier to employment was also highlighted by a number of witnesses:

If there is one major thing you could do to allow people with mental health problems to access employment it would be to change the benefits system. People are in a situation where if they go off benefits they will not be able to pay for their accommodation. *Tony Coggins, Lewisham and Guy's Mental Health Trust*

People who receive Disability Living Allowance really lose out if they try to start work. Then there is mortgage relief, which tapers much faster than housing benefit relief, so if you've got a mortgage you can't consider working unless you're going to earn really quite a substantial salary. *Rachel Perkins, South West London and St George's Mental Health NHS Trust*

People diagnosed with schizophrenia are amongst the poorest members of society. They are dependent on disability allowances. If they are able to work in a sheltered facility, they cannot earn more than £15 per week, the so-called therapeutic earnings limit, without having the amount deducted from their allowance. *Julian Leff, Institute of Psychiatry*

The theme of disclosure of psychiatric history in all areas of life ran throughout the Inquiry proceedings. Many witnesses pointed to the difficulties and dangers of disclosure at work, while others, particularly employers, pointed to the problems with lack of disclosure. All human resources and equal opportunities policies are driven by the information gained from self-disclosure by employees. If no one is 'coming out' about having mental health problems then it may be harder for enlightened employers to give the help that may be needed:

If an employee tells us they are suffering from a mental illness, or if at recruitment stage they tell us they would like support because they've had a mental illness, then we will keep that information and act on it. If they don't wish to tell us, then we can't provide any services that help or support. *Chrissie Lawson, Tesco*

Our audits are done on a statistical basis. Every six months we collate various figures to produce employee profiles. One of the problems in this area is that obviously it is done on a self-certification basis. We ask people if they have a disability, and not everyone will want to tell us. *Gale Issitt, HSBC*

The Disability Discrimination Act (DDA) (see Glossary) was seen as a very positive step:

It's an opportunity to bring into the open the whole discussion of disability, and that includes mental health. It's an education process for employers, and the DDA is genuinely helping in that process. *Sue Wallis, The Boots Company*

But many witnesses were unsure of its efficacy:

Mental health issues may be covered under the Disability Discrimination Act. But the DDA needs to be looked at quite hard as to whether it actually has any teeth. *Gale Issitt, HSBC*

There are concerns about the current lack of a Commission to monitor the implementation of the DDA. *Sophie Corlett, Skill – National Bureau for Students with Disabilities*

Witnesses were also unsure whether the DDA took sufficient account of mental health problems as opposed to physical or sensory disabilities:

One of the big weaknesses of the definition of disability in the DDA is on the mental health side, because you have to have a major effect on your day-to-day activities. Those day-to-day activities are primarily defined in terms of physical or sensory impairments, so it can be difficult to qualify. One fairly notorious case was somebody diagnosed with schizophrenia who had just been released from hospital. He was found not to be disabled under the DDA because the tribunal was impressed that he was capable of living on his own and capable of working – despite the fact that he'd been sacked. *Caroline Gooding, Employers' Forum on Disability*

Education and training

Lack of access to educational and training opportunities is another key aspect of social exclusion. Many witnesses stressed the piecemeal and *ad hoc* arrangements within education for people with mental health problems:

> Equality of opportunity and the elimination of prejudice and discrimination should not be issues of individual mission or academic autonomy. Equality and lack of discrimination are foundation stones of the delivery of quality and academic rigour. Yet practice within higher education institutions varies greatly; some institutions have comprehensive and effective provision for disabled students. In many places, however, the quality of a student's experience depends on the commitment of individual departments or members of staff, and the availability of funding at any particular time. *Sophie Corlett, Skill – National Bureau for Students with Disabilities*

Poor education provision for students with mental health difficulties has been noted in recent reports:

> The Further Education Funding Council in England carried out a review of its provision, published in the Tomlinson report, *Inclusive Learning,* in 1996 [Further Education Funding Council 1996]. The primary principle was that further education needed to move towards a more inclusive, student-centred approach. The report found that certain groups are currently under-represented in further education: people of all ages with profound and multiple disabilities, young people with emotional and behavioural difficulties, and adults with mental health problems. *Sophie Corlett, Skill – National Bureau for Students with Disabilities*

One of the other major criticisms of the DDA was that it did not cover education:

The DDA has led to some improvements in the opportunities for disabled people, and it is regrettable that education was excluded from the Act. Students are turned down from courses on the basis that they have had mental health difficulties. It is assumed they will not be able to hack it on the course. This is particularly the case for professional courses such as teacher training, medicine or nursing. The irony is that if these people were already trained and applying for work in these fields, then employers, under the DDA, would have a responsibility to look at the person as an individual and not to discriminate unfairly. *Sophie Corlett, Skill – National Bureau for Students with Disabilities*

Lack of knowledge and understanding, and outright prejudice, were the barriers many people with mental health problems faced in trying to enter the education system:

Some staff within college environments have very negative attitudes; the fear, the prejudice comes up, with the idea of the 'mad axeman'. Then there's the lack of knowledge. Mention mental health problems and what tends to happen is either people say, 'Oh yes, we've got some classes for people with learning difficulties'. Or they direct you to the disabilities officer, so that you're immediately marginalised. *Jan Turnbull, Coventry Social Services*

Recent emphasis within higher education on the needs and abilities of students with disabilities has focused on physical and environmental barriers. Further attention should be given to the needs of students with mental health problems as part of higher education's expressed aim to broaden access. *Jill Manthorpe and Nicky Stanley, University of Hull (written evidence)*

Again, most witnesses to the Inquiry were united in feeling that 'mainstreaming' was fundamental to social inclusion, and that the creation of separate facilities for people with mental health problems, in education, in employment or in other areas of society was counter-productive and exclusionary. Parallels were drawn with the exclusion from mainstream education of children with physical disabilities or learning difficulties:

The entire education system is underpinned by an unaware but deeply entrenched policy of segregation, based on totally false concepts of 'ability' and 'disability'. The eugenic philosophies of the past have shaped laws, services and attitudes that live on through the whole concept of 'special education'. The antidote is reality! Disabled and non-disabled people meeting, especially when young, and being supported to live and learn together. *Micheline Mason, Alliance for Inclusive Education*

We've got to draw lessons from across the board. Canadian research looking at children with support needs who were being supported in mainstream schools (but who would traditionally end up in special schools in Britain), found not only that those children learn better but the others in the classroom learn better too. *Peter Bates, National Development Team*

In addition to attitudes of staff, tutors and other students and trainees, there are a number of practical barriers preventing people with mental health problems from accessing training and education:

The problems and gaps in the services are very varied: transport problems, benefit difficulties, issues of confidentiality. Sometimes it's just the sheer size of campuses; if you've got mental health problems and you're feeling anxious, then just to go through the college door is such a huge step. This isn't recognised, that the first step through the door can be like doing a degree for someone else. If you need a support worker to sit with you because you're anxious, then that help should be there. Just as if you were in a wheelchair and you needed help from someone to push you through the doors. *Jan Turnbull, Coventry Social Services*

Disabled students' allowances are not available to part-time students, which is how many people with mental health problems may want to enter the education system. The lack of funding for part-time and postgraduate students, for those on certain courses such as nursing or occupational therapy, for those who are forced to change their mode of study because of illness, or for those who take time out from a course, continues to create barriers for many people. It would be relatively inexpensive to remedy this difficulty.

Under the modular system in higher education you've got an exam every six months, coursework to hand in. If you miss one deadline the whole thing can fall apart. Rather than being able to drop out for a time, and then go back when health has improved, students often have to drop out altogether. This increasing 'flexibility' in the system, in fact, often does not help people with mental health problems at all.

With National Vocational Qualifications (NVQs) for example, the outcomes have to be reached. If you don't reach your outcomes as a trainee within the allotted time then the person that's placed you doesn't get their money. So then they're reluctant to take people on who may seem to be a poor investment. *Sophie Corlett, Skill – National Bureau for Students with Disabilities*

The mental health of all students also needs to be looked at in a broader way:

While much attention has been focused on student suicide, other problems and issues connected to mental health have been far less visible. Further work is required to address the areas of suicide and self-harm, but also to identify other outcomes and preventative strategies. Similarly, students' mental health problems are much more diverse than the stereotypical picture of an undergraduate facing examination stress. The particular needs of mature students, part-time students, international students and those from minority ethnic groups should be researched and addressed. *Jill Manthorpe and Nicky Stanley, University of Hull (written evidence)*

As one witness commented:

The Dearing Report stated that one of the four main purposes of higher education is 'to play a major role in shaping a democratic, civilised, inclusive society'. To take on such an ambitious role, higher education must display a greater commitment to becoming more civilised and inclusive. *Sophie Corlett, Skill – National Bureau for Students with Disabilities*

Daily living: access to goods, services and social networks

Discriminatory and prejudiced attitudes have their effect throughout all aspects of people's lives. Seemingly straightforward everyday tasks such as shopping, or applying for a mortgage or insurance, can be made unpleasant or impossible. And the segregated nature of mental health services themselves effectively cuts off service users from the rest of society.

Previous research has noted the difficulties people with mental health problems have in gaining insurance (see section 1.1 p. 8), and this issue was brought up by several of the witnesses:

> When you want to organise a mortgage and get life cover, all the medical history that is in the GP's notes is sent to the insurance company. They say 'Oh this guy's been in hospital, on lithium, all these other drugs, let's put a loading on.' I've got a 60 per cent loading on my insurance cover. I've written to the company to say that I have always disputed the diagnosis that led to all that psychiatric treatment. They said they would review it after five years. So for five years I'm paying the premium of someone who smokes 30 cigarettes a day. *Tom O'Brien, general practitioner*

> I was refused insurance on the basis of my 'medical history', the only significant part of which is my mental health problems. Prior to these appearing in my records I had no difficulty obtaining insurance. Ever since I started working, way back when, I've always had a disability insurance policy, so that if I was unable to work I would still be paid a salary. I'd been promoted a lot, so I asked to extend the insurance. They said, 'Certainly, just fill in this form.' I filled in the form and they said, 'Not on your life'. Despite evidence from my chief executive as to my competence, from my psychiatrist as to the stability of my condition and that it does not prevent me from working, they have completely refused to consider me unless I 'get better'.
>
> It seems to me that if the only conditions under which insurance companies will deal with people who have mental health problems is if they cease to have them anymore – even if they are capable of working – then that is unreasonable discrimination. *Rachel Perkins, South West London and St George's Mental Health NHS Trust*

I know what response I will get if I talk of my mental health problems. When I fill in an insurance form I have to put down about my depression. I got refusals from the three companies I tried. *Jo, mental health service user*

Several witnesses made analogies between the workings of anti-gay prejudice and the workings of prejudice towards people with mental health problems. This was highlighted in various ways, including the area of insurance:

There are problems for gay people about insurance of all sorts – holiday, home, mortgages, life. The problems stem from the assumptions insurers make, solely on the basis of a label, about people's lifestyle and behaviour. This seems to operate in a similar way to the assumptions they make about psychiatric labels. *Tom Lawson, Terence Higgins Trust*

Problems can arise in the most mundane tasks of everyday life:

One service user wanted to start weight-training at a local gym. He went in and met the trainer in the foyer. The guy asked him if he was on any medication – meaning for heart problems or other physical health conditions that might make him flake out during exercise. But what happened was that they ended up talking about injecting psychotropic medication, in a public foyer. The whole sports centre needed to learn better practice for confidentiality. *Peter Bates, National Development Team*

There's a whole minor set of things I have never really thought about until I experienced my own mental health difficulties. Things like the sidelong looks you get from pharmacists when you go along with a prescription for psychotropic medication.

And then there's the problem with never being allowed to get a headache: if you take a prescription for antidepressants to a chemist, they will not let you simultaneously buy paracetamol or aspirin. I now have one chemist I go to for my psychiatric medication, and one for everything else. It became too silly otherwise. *Rachel Perkins, South West London and St George's Mental Health NHS Trust*

I know of mental health service users who have experienced unwelcoming responses from bank staff when they have tried to open an account. Demands for specific forms of ID are a real sticking point. Passports, council tax bills and driving licences are the banks' most favoured forms of ID. Each of these may pose a problem for service users, most particularly the driving licence, as many users do not have the funds for owning a car or are prohibited from driving because of medication.

Some places accept letters from employers as ID, but the rates of employment for service users mean this is useless for the vast majority. Bills that give a name and address are acceptable to some banks, but people who live in staffed or shared accommodation may not have access to these. Some banks and building societies accept a reference on NHS headed paper, but this raises issues of confidentiality and immediately marks the person out as different. *Peter Bates, National Development Team*

Social exclusion is a 'holistic' process; exclusion from one aspect of society almost inevitably has a knock-on effect on all other areas of life. Many witnesses drew attention to the highly stigmatised status of users of mental health services in contemporary Britain:

Social inclusion must come down surely to somewhere to live, something to do, someone to love. It's as simple – and as complicated – as that. And there are all kinds of barriers to people with mental health problems having those three things. *Charles Fraser, St Mungo's*

The biggest problem to overcome is the exclusion psychologically of people who members of the public see as different from themselves. As professionals we have maintained that view by creating asylums. We are trying to disband them, we're trying to change that view, but there are still professional attitudes of paternalism, benign or otherwise, that continue to maintain that exclusion. *Julian Leff, Institute of Psychiatry*

Psychiatry has created such fear of people who have mental health problems. Those who have had mental health problems have been traditionally regarded as the lowest of the low. Unemployment, social isolation, poverty, homelessness, stigma, contempt and fear surround people with mental health problems like a shroud. It is easier to live in society with a prison record than a psychiatric record. *Hywel Davies, Pembrokeshire Hearing Voices Group*

We structure our whole society through this massive, complicated 'national conversation'. This is expressed in cultural terms through the media, through artistic activity, community events of all kinds. One of the first prerequisites of the marginalisation, and eventually demonisation, of social groups is to deny them the opportunity of being involved in this national conversation: mental health service users are being excluded from this process. *Francois Matarasso, Comedia*

Many service users who gave evidence felt that their diagnosis made them 'non-citizens', with no rights, no credibility and no redress, from either the state, mental health services or other members of society:

Everyone has the right to freedom of opinion and expression, but I often elect not to exercise that right because of the consequences. Any display of emotion above the normal stiff English upper lip is considered an illness. In a society unwilling or unable to listen, freedom of speech is not only useless but dangerous. *Jo, mental health service user*

Psychiatry takes a very dim view of spiritual things. They see it as tantamount to mental illness. A psychiatrist actually said to me: 'If you don't give up that religion stuff you'll be back in here again.' *Tom O'Brien, general practitioner*

Immediately after I was admitted to a psychiatric hospital I lost custody of my children. I had worked as a registered children's nurse, brought up my children on my own, done the best I could. But as soon as I was admitted to a psychiatric hospital I could no longer be trusted with my children. *Lorraine Lawson, mental health service user*

As someone who has suffered mental distress, my human rights are something I fight daily to have recognised. When I sought an injunction against a man who has been violent to me for 15 years, I was subject to psychiatric reports to establish my credibility as a witness. *Jo, mental health service user*

I've been abused in the street. I've had my house broken into twelve times and had a knife put through the door. All in an effort to try and drive me out. And I'm the one who's supposed to be nasty and violent. *Lorraine Lawson, mental health service user*

A number of witnesses pointed to the power of the media in shaping and reinforcing people's fearful and prejudiced reactions to those with mental health problems:

There must be a change in the way people with mental health problems are portrayed in the media. Only the other week I was watching TV and it showed a young schizophrenic and I thought to myself, 'He's going to kill someone because they never make programmes where schizophrenics don't kill people.' And sure enough he did. *Lorraine Lawson, mental health service user*

During my research, service users have commented that news media articles are often alarmist and provide an unbalanced view with no statistical counterbalance. For example, homicides among mentally ill people are viewed without reference to the suicides that are so much more common and say so much more about their plight. *Mike Birch, Falmouth College of Arts*

In a recent survey of public attitudes to mental disorders, 71 per cent considered people with schizophrenia to be a danger to others. This perception has undoubtedly been heightened by the manner in which the media highlights homicides committed by the mentally ill, and by the portrayal of mentally ill people in film and TV drama. *Julian Leff, Institute of Psychiatry*

The schizophrenic identity is portrayed as an outlaw culture. It produces the stereotype of a dangerous and fearsome other, raising parallels with how other social groups have been oppressed in the media; similarities with minority ethnic groups, homosexuals and other marginalised groups abound. *Mike Birch, Falmouth College of Arts*

Amongst those with mental health problems, some groups are subject to additional, compounding exclusion or discrimination on other grounds:

> I regard people in prison who have serious mental health problems as the most excluded in society. The treatment of people with serious mental illness in prison is an absolute disgrace. When you go into prison you not only lose your rights as a citizen, but you also lose your rights to health care. *Lionel Joyce, Newcastle NHS Trust*

> We set up our project because as much as people with mental health problems experience prejudice in many ways, there are particular difficulties experienced by black and ethnic minorities, because they have racism to face and because the health services are not geared to their needs. *Marilyn Bryan, Awetu Black Mental Health Project*

> Mental wellbeing in Britain's black communities has to be understood in a wider context that includes the experience of discrimination in various forms. Discrimination is very real and has a material impact. It is still the case that black people live in particular urban areas, which tend to be in major metropolitan cities. These urban areas tend to be in those parts of the city where the housing stock is oldest, the most high-rise blocks are situated, and the crime rates and unemployment rates are highest. This is part of the structure in which black communities live, in which they experience the stresses of daily living and the stresses that impact on mental wellbeing.
>
> The experience of poverty is reflected in the uptake of social services. So for example you see black people being represented in local authority care systems, but black families being under-represented in family support. Similarly, black old people are less likely to be receiving home care services than their white counterparts. All this must be part of the background when thinking about mental health and black people. *Jabeer Butt, Race Equality Unit*

> We work with many people from the Arabic community whose immigration or asylum status has not been cleared. Quite a lot are suffering from mental health problems, or their partners are. They

live in poor housing, and this aggravates their mental ill-health. Racism is a big problem, not just in wider society but in institutions as well. People are being discriminated against, so they are not accessing mainstream services. One of our clients was told by her GP that he'd pay her fare back if she went home, simply for the fact that she wears a *hajib* [see Glossary]. *Samira Ben Omar, Al-Hasaniya Moroccan Women's Centre*

I have seen many asylum seekers, particularly young Somali men, committing suicide in their first years in the UK. Inequality or discrimination exists in the statutory sector, and this becomes acute when general phobias, political motivations and Islamophobia are combined. There is a great lack of understanding about the Muslim perspective. *Shafiqur Rahman, Royal London Hospitals Trust Chaplaincy*

Once again there was criticism of the 'ghettoisation' of those with mental health problems and the services provided for them:

If you ask long-term service users who they know, who they have in their social networks, a lot of people who have been in the system a long time produce a very short list. If you take out relatives, staff and other service users, the list falls to zero. *Peter Bates, National Development Team*

Even when people are moved into the so-called community, what you find is, for example, work opportunities are sheltered opportunities, in which people are still protected by a *cordon sanitaire* of professionals. They do not come into contact with 'ordinary members of the public'. *Julian Leff, Institute of Psychiatry*

Some say that the lack of social networks for people with mental health problems is due to the people themselves – that there is something wrong with their confidence for example. Others say it is because there is something wrong with the community – that is it is stigmatising and prejudiced. I think it is because there is something wrong with the services. In my view, traditional services have ghettoised users. It is possible to stick people in community settings where they remain powerless, poor and lonely. That is not a lot better than the old ghetto. I think mock reformers can subtly transform the old hierarchies into a new location, so that staff still make all the decisions. *Peter Bates, National Development Team*

I'm not sure the lessons of institutionalisation have been learned. Every small town has a clutch of residential homes, often situated in large houses in spacious grounds. In the homes are people whose contact with the 'outside world' is limited and in some cases non-existent. I would describe this as community institutionalisation, and it is no nearer a system of integrated care than the old psychiatric hospitals. *Arthur Hawes, Archdeacon of Lincoln*

Putting 'types' of people all together in institutions and pretending an alternative and equally valid community has been formed does not work. They just get to be meaningless together. *Micheline Mason, Alliance for Inclusive Education*

Witnesses drew attention to the ways in which social exclusion can also affect the family and carers of those with mental health problems:

Carers of the mentally ill also get trapped by the discrimination. They become ashamed, they won't talk to their friends and relatives so they lose their natural support systems. They stop inviting people into their home, and they stop taking the ill person out, so they become isolated in their own little castle. One way to address this is relatives' support groups, but these are very, very rare within the NHS. *Julian Leff, Institute of Psychiatry*

Sometimes the role of the carer is affected by social exclusion. It becomes difficult for them to have a life. Carers can become very much involved and responsible, and of course that can be very problematic. We provide direct support to carers, in an attempt to enable the carers to allow the service user to determine their own care. But frequently the carer can become over-involved, and there is an unfortunate dynamic. *Simon Morris, Jewish Care*

Mental health services

Many Inquiry witnesses saw aspects of mental health services as part of the problem as much as part of the solution. A common thread of evidence was that engagement with mental health services, while intended to ameliorate distress, could actually increase it.

Some witnesses felt that the diagnosis of mental illness given by psychiatrists caused more distress than the original problem:

> We run projects where we know the individuals are actively in flight from treatments, because of the very negative experiences they have had of the NHS or social services. *Charles Fraser, St Mungo's*

> The psychiatric services treat you badly, and I think they are partly guilty for the way society then treats you as well. *Lorraine Lawson, mental health service user*

> I've been under the care of psychiatrists since 1995. At times I have chosen not to see a psychiatrist because they can't actually do much about my distress. My distress is caused by my past experiences, and all psychiatry tries to do is at best treat the symptoms with medication, and at worst incarcerate me against my will. *Jo, mental health service user*

> The big problem with psychiatry is the labelling. Once you enter the psychiatric system it's a downward spiral. Psychiatrists' notes generate more psychiatrists' notes. You get this label, this diagnosis, and if you disagree with it you lack insight. If you continue to disagree you just build up the notes, and the more notes there are, the more the psychiatrists think there is a problem. You are in a no-win situation. *Tom O'Brien, general practitioner*

> The principal enemy of the 'lunatic' is psychiatric orthodoxy. I do think people need to be educated about the past of psychiatry – how it has labelled groups such as single mothers, lesbians and gay men, slaves who tried to escape, all as 'mentally ill'. Psychiatry labelled me a 'schizophrenic' in 1983. I was unaware of the ramifications of the term, the fear it inspired in others. I told friends about it and they cut me out of their lives; it's still a sore point. *Hywel Davies, Pembrokeshire Hearing Voices Group*

> Diagnostic terms are so powerful. It is particularly damaging to talk about 'a schizophrenic' as opposed to 'a person with a diagnosis of schizophrenia'. The noun 'schizophrenic' labels someone in such a

powerful way; it says that this person is less human, less than a full member of society. The fundamental point here is that the discrimination people experience arises *because of the diagnosis,* not as a result of the condition itself. *Simon Foster, Mind*

Several witnesses drew specific attention to the adverse effects of psychiatric medication as being in themselves the cause of distress to users and hostility from others:

The unwanted side-effects of psychiatric medication are also a great concern. I know someone who has tardive dyskinesia [see Glossary]. His feet shake, his hands shake – and it's not the result of mental distress, it's the medication he was given. So psychiatry has actually further damaged someone who was already mentally vulnerable. *Hywel Davies, Pembrokeshire Hearing Voices Group*

Side-effects of psychiatric drugs are in themselves causes of discrimination. If you see a person shuffling down the road with a fixed stare and immobile limbs you know there is something wrong with them – and this is what a lot of our treatments do to people with severe mental illness. A new generation of drugs that do not create these side-effects is available. But many health authorities will not fund them, on the grounds they are too expensive. So one of the founding principles of the NHS, the right to best treatment, is not applied to people with severe mental illness. *Julian Leff, Institute of Psychiatry*

Some of the residents living in our hostels suffer negative side-effects from the use of prescribed drugs. Staff are very concerned about this. We advocate on behalf of residents reporting side-effects to doctors. *Charles Fraser, St Mungo's*

Often ward staff don't actually have the knowledge to give people the information they need about drugs – both their potential benefits and their potential problems – in order to make an informed decision. I routinely insist on seeing the *British National Formulary* [publication listing all drugs prescribed in the UK, their uses, recommended doses and adverse effects] before being prescribed something. And very often people feel threatened when the patient knows more than they do. *Rachel Perkins, South West London and St George's Mental Health NHS Trust*

I was in hospital voluntarily, being prescribed some antidepressants, and they didn't agree with me, making me more irritable and also making me nauseous. I said to my psychiatrist, 'These drugs are making me feel bad.' He said, 'It's your mental illness that is making you feel bad, not the drugs.' This went on for weeks and I felt worse and worse.

Then I had a bad conversation with my ex-husband, I was furious and I shouted a threat at him and a nurse overheard; then I was carted off to the secure unit. I was sectioned under the Mental Health Act and I was there for four months. All the time I was there I was told I should not use the word 'angry'. I mean it's a normal human emotion isn't it? But I was told, 'You're going to be locked away in your room for longer if you use the word angry.'

When I came off this particular drug I was fine. *Lorraine Lawson, mental health service user*

In one form or another almost every witness to the Inquiry was concerned with the excessively medicalised nature of psychiatric services, at the expense of addressing social and economic issues:

Traditional services have ghettoised users. They have severed their links with other citizens. In order for services to stop promoting exclusion, they must stop promoting containment. Mental health services, both statutory and voluntary, must begin to recognise that users are citizens first, friends and loved ones second, employees and enthusiasts third, and users of mental health services only fourth or fifth. And the absence of a real rallying point for mental health inclusion means that what good examples there are get neglected rather than celebrated. *Peter Bates, National Development Team*

We run residential services – our perspective on mental illness is entirely social-services linked. We are the cinderella of social services, let alone the health services, and we find ourselves being talked down to by health professionals. In addition, the bureaucracy of the NHS is utterly impenetrable; we find it impossible to find our way around the health services, and clearly this can only aggravate the divisions and gaps between services and the social exclusion of our residents and clients. *Charles Fraser, St Mungo's*

As Sayce (1998) has pointed out:

Clinicians need to understand mental health problems *in relation* to the disabling effects of discrimination. Research has shown that even where diagnosis leads to effective treatment of symptoms, stigma, including discrimination, continues, as do users' strategies for dealing with it. These strategies include withdrawal and not risking applying for jobs for fear of rejection – both of which can sometimes be construed as further evidence of symptoms. Continuing stigma is associated with recurrence of mental health problems. This means that treating the symptoms is an insufficient clinical strategy; they are likely to continue and recur until discrimination is addressed.

This was echoed by many witnesses' comments on mental health services' inability to provide specialist and appropriate *systems of support* where they are needed. Witnesses drew particular attention to this issue in relation to minority ethnic groups, people with physical disabilities, and lesbian, gay and bisexual people:

We need to look at particular excluded groups. We work with young men from the African-Caribbean community, who are disproportionately represented in both the mental health and prison systems. We are concerned about the need to create culturally appropriate services for these young men who are reluctant to approach traditional services.

We are also concerned about self-harm amongst young Asian women. There are complex reasons why people from these communities may not approach mental health services, and culturally sensitive outreach work is sorely needed. *Alistair Cox, 42nd Street*

Mental health work in Britain has become obsessed with trying to explain high rates of treatment in certain communities. The literature always concentrates on some aspect of the African-

Caribbean community and why it is more highly represented in certain forms of treatment. Many of the explanations are pathological; they range from the stress of migrating to Britain to excessive smoking of marijuana to inherent psychological traits. Nobody seems to have quite grasped that if you can't replicate the findings then they must be flawed, or there are problems with diagnoses.

The obsession with medicalised views of mental health in black communities means there is little attention paid to support services. Some Leeds research found that black people being assessed with mental health problems were more likely to be offered drugs than counselling. When a counselling service for black people was set up, demand was extensive.

Caribbean young men have the highest rates of unemployment in this country; this inevitably has an impact on your mental wellbeing, it inevitably puts stresses on the way you survive and develop. There is a tendency to not join together the issues that face black people and then understand how that has an overall impact on services. So for example when Christopher Clunis comes to the public's attention, nobody looks at what has happened to his family, the failure of the mental health service system to find his sister who had been taking care of him. *Jabeer Butt, Race Equality Unit*

Black people with mental health difficulties have been excluded from mental health services. There aren't services geared specifically to their needs, and often they haven't been aware of what general services have been available and so have not accessed mental health care through, for example, GPs. *Marilyn Bryan, Awetu Black Mental Health Project*

A lot of our clients, who are from Morocco and other Arabic-speaking countries, are experiencing mental ill-health and are simply not accessing services. They fall through the net and receive no help. For example, one client who was hearing voices was going regularly to her GP. He kept sending her to an ear specialist. Eventually she came to us and we found her a psychiatrist from her own cultural background, who understood and was able to diagnose her. *Samira Ben Omar, Al-Hasaniya Moroccan Women's Centre*

Distress is often expressed in culturally specific ways that can sometimes be misinterpreted by mainstream agencies. We provide alcohol advice services to members of the black community, whose patterns of alcohol use are significantly different from the white community. For example, a significant factor is that clients are ashamed of their drinking, are covert drinkers and present as very independent, smart and well kept. This can lead some agencies to minimise the problem. Also, a lack of recognition of alcohol and substance misuse contributes to the overdiagnosis of schizophrenia amongst African-Caribbean people. *Alcohol Recovery Project (written evidence)*

There is a lack of appreciation of context in psychiatry. For example I have a perforated eardrum, so I speak quite loudly. I also speak quite quickly, and I think psychiatrists then interpret that as some sign of 'mania'. Then I'm Irish, I'm an ethnic minority in a sense, we express ourselves differently, much more upfront. I think this was interpreted as part of an 'illness' as well. *Tom O'Brien, general practitioner*

Some people in the lesbian, gay and bisexual population have had serious breakdowns, may have been hospitalised as a result and subsequently felt alienated and stigmatised within mental health systems. The young gay people we work with speak of uniformly negative experiences with formal psychiatric services. *Alistair Cox, 42nd Street*

Deaf people [those either born deaf or who become deaf] have historically received appalling treatment by psychiatry. They have been incorrectly diagnosed as having learning disabilities or as having psychotic disorders. Sometimes this has been due to a total lack of understanding of British Sign Language (BSL). Psychiatrists do not understand BSL, so deaf people are forced to communicate by writing, and since BSL is grammatically unconnected to English, the sometimes poor written English of deaf people has been used to diagnose them as thought disordered.

Deaf people do have mental health problems, just like hearing people, but they cannot access the services. Where are the means of access for deaf people to primary care, to counselling, to CPNs, to mental health promotion? My research has shown quite high levels of distress amongst the deaf population, but hardly anyone is attempting to include them in service provision. *Sharon Ridgeway, National Centre for Mental Health and Deafness*

Some witnesses spoke of the success of some minority groups in setting up culturally specific services. However, they drew attention to the ways in which this could impact negatively on people with mental health problems, for example by causing statutory services to withdraw prematurely, so isolating users from mainstream provision, or by exposing users to situations where their mental health difficulties were seen as very stigmatising:

There is no doubt that discrimination against Jewish people does occur in this country. I think this is one of the reasons that organisations such as Jewish Care exist. We have always prided ourselves in being able to 'look after our own'. However, there is a downside, and that is that we provide care in a very paternalistic way, our systems tending to be patriarchal and hierarchical, and the services given in a benevolent manner, with issues like user-involvement, until very recently, trailing a long way behind.

Added to this, the Jewish community, like others, excludes people with mental health problems; mental illness isn't often talked about. Within the ultra-orthodox community, for example, there is an even more closed approach to understanding or working with mental health issues.

There is also the issue of statutory services 'handing over'. Because we are in a sense a holistic provider of services there is a feeling that once someone is in contact with us then they are taken care of. Once someone slips out of the net and becomes a regular user of our services, then the CPN, the social worker, the psychiatrist are all too happy to pull back and let us provide. There is real difficulty in accessing and keeping statutory services involved with our provision. Then people can find themselves suffering the double isolation of having mental health problems and being isolated within the Jewish community. This then makes reintegration into mainstream society doubly difficult. *Simon Morris, Jewish Care*

The tendency within mental health services and also general health services to exclude people regarded as 'difficult' – for example people diagnosed with co-existing substance misuse and mental health problems – has been noted by researchers: 'The many problems and needs of this group require input from many agencies. Since this group can be so challenging to engage, and hard to keep contact with, it can be tempting for agencies to deny their role, and to try to shift the responsibility to another agency' (Sainsbury Centre for Mental Health 1998). Witnesses to the Inquiry also commented on this process with regard to general (non-psychiatric) health care:

> Discrimination within the NHS is something we are particularly interested in. This was drawn to our attention because of the fact that general practitioners are protected by regulations if they discriminate against patients by striking them off their practice lists. I would like to underline the fact that whilst the Mental Health Patients Charter refers to a right not to be discriminated against, this has neither authority nor remedy in law, or in any procedures of the NHS. We are concerned about the discrimination practised by GPs who remove 'heavy' patients – people with mental health problems, the elderly, those with learning disabilities, drug users – from their lists. *South Tyneside Community Health Council (written evidence)*

> There are a lot of people who have been given a psychiatric diagnosis, who when they go and see their GP with what they think is a medical condition the doctor will say, 'Go away, it's all in your head.' When I was in a psychiatric hospital I started to get bad stomach pains; when I complained of these the staff assumed I just wanted attention. After I got out of hospital the condition carried on, and by then I was scared to get it looked at in case they sectioned me again. Eventually the pain was so bad I had to get it checked out, and it turned out I had a large ovarian cyst. *Lorraine Lawson, mental health service user*

Another area of particular concern to witnesses was the treatment of adolescents and young adults (14–25) within mainstream services. The appropriate response to a first experience of extreme distress is crucial if the downward spiral of mental ill-health and compounding social exclusion of which many witnesses spoke is not to be triggered. But at the age when many people are most vulnerable, they find themselves in limbo between child and adult mental health services:

> Something awful happens in the attempt to move young people from child and adolescent mental health services into adult ones. It really is a dire situation that people aged 14, 15, 16 end up in a no-person's land, with no one really taking responsibility. Then they often find themselves on adult psychiatric wards and find that a really intolerable experience, a time of great difficulty and apprehension that can be so damaging.
>
> We lose people at that crucial point, and I think we really need to look at specialised community-based services for 14–25 year olds that allow people to grow at their own pace, to find their own understanding of themselves and move into independence. These services need to be doing prevention work and mental health promotion work, as well as being able to respond appropriately to already existing severe mental distress. *Alistair Cox, 42nd Street*

> I was a very naïve 17 year old, living on my own with no support, trying to cope with having been abused as a child, looking after my sisters, holding down a job and keeping my flat and bills in order. After spending a very difficult Christmas in my rented room I took an overdose that resulted in me being taken into hospital and then into an acute adult psychiatric ward. I wasn't even there one day. Someone tried to smash a window because she was so distressed and I was absolutely terrified. I'd never even heard of mental illness and I had no idea that psychiatric hospitals still existed. I was so frightened I went home that day.
>
> A few months later I went into hospital again. I was desperate. No one explained to me what was going to happen in hospital, my treatments or what exactly depression was. The only verbal contact I had was when I was given medication. I also had ECT; I didn't know what that was until very recently. I didn't need to be shut away somewhere where I had nothing to do. I needed someone to respect me and listen to what I was saying my problem was and what I thought the answer was. If they'd done that I could have saved them a lot of hospital fees. *Jo, mental health service user*

According to recent research by the Mental Health Foundation, the majority of children with mental health problems never reach specialist services, and inter-agency collaboration, even where well executed, is proving insufficient to the challenge of delivering speedy and effective response for vulnerable young people. In addition, enormous stigma is attached to mental illness by both the children themselves and parents and carers; it is likely therefore that help would be sought earlier if provided through entry points that do not have a 'mental health' label (Mental Health Foundation 1999).

Several witnesses pointed out how the inappropriate compartmentalising of mental health services based on diagnosis rather than support needs caused particular difficulties for certain groups of people, including homeless people and people with co-existing substance misuse and mental health problems:

> As a rule of thumb, we take the view that we are working with groups of people who are casualties of social policy failure. Care in the community is one of the great misnomers of our time. It is meant to be the route through which we provide services structured in accordance with need, rather than being provision- or funding-led. Significantly, homelessness is not considered to be a needs-dimension when community living assessments are carried out. This is, in our view, due to two related factors: first, local authorities in London have been wary of committing themselves to provision for homeless people with mental illness out of anxiety that it will serve as a kind of magnet. Second, care in the community as a policy has always had at its heart assumptions about local residency, or at least demonstrable local connections. It's quite clear to us that if you are homeless you don't actually belong to this community. The people with whom we work are in the community, but they sure as hell aren't of the community, and that is symptomatic institutional exclusion.
>
> There is an additional genuine difficulty with people with 'dual diagnosis' [see Glossary] or multiple needs. As with most disadvantages and disabilities they are over-represented amongst our client group, where a mental illness can mask a drug problem or vice versa. Not only does assessment become notoriously difficult, but there is an inadequacy of available response. This leads to problems with generalist service provision at a street or emergency level; generalist hostels may take people off the streets, but inevitably problems arise when you have people with different

needs rubbing up against each other in a very uncontrolled way. We are passionate advocates of specialist segregated provision at emergency level, leading on to more integrated care later on. *Charles Fraser, St Mungo's*

There is a group that is falling through the health and social services net. Probably the chief characteristic is that they have multiple problems: as well as being mentally vulnerable they have drug or alcohol problems, housing difficulties, family discord. Mainstream social services have focused for the last ten to fifteen years on very specific people. If you don't fall into that group, you're excluded or even discriminated against. This excluded group is predominantly male, and early 30s; they are mentally vulnerable people who come into contact with the police. They are primarily minor offenders – drunk and disorderly, breach of the peace, shoplifting. They are known to the local social and health services, but the services have not been able to engage with them over the long-term. *Toby Seddon, Revolving Doors Agency*

The impact on provision of mental health services of neighbourhood opposition, including 'not in my back yard' (nimby) campaigns has been shown to be significant. Several witnesses saw nimbyism as perhaps one of the most graphic and brutal manifestations of social exclusion:

We must challenge the exclusionary attitudes of those in society who don't allow mental health facilities in their neighbourhood, who wage the war against the hostel. When we asked people about what happens if they complain about being excluded from their local community, they said that they didn't complain for fear of being thought trouble-makers, or because they wouldn't be believed. I want to make a plea for the right to live in the community, but as long as that community operates justly and reasonably. *Arthur Hawes, Archdeacon of Lincoln*

We have noticed that nothing revives a moribund residents' or tenants' association as instantly as the prospect of St Mungo's turning up on their doorstep. [St Mungo's provides services for single homeless people, and specialises in mental health.] The sort of responses we get from the community are based on the basic premise that 'All these people are serial drug abusers, criminally insane and child molesters'. Then we get a variety of lines following from that premise: 'Why don't you buy up the houses next to the politicians and put them in there and see how the MPs like it?' Or 'Our community is a good one and it is completely unacceptable to let these ne'er-do-wells into the area.' Or another, more subtle one that we notice more and more: 'This area is a sink of vice and drugs and prostitution, and how could you as a reputable charity contemplate putting your services here?'

In the homelessness field there is a DoE initiative called the Rough Sleepers Initiative, which has encouraged the establishment of not just shelters but longer-term arrangements. The DoE is also responsible for planning regulations. So you see one arm of the DoE promoting the establishment of housing solutions, and the other arm supporting attempts to prevent its establishment. It's chaos. *Charles Fraser, St Mungo's*

And it is not just local residents who wage nimby campaigns. Witnesses pointed to the part played by local councillors and politicians, who are often guilty themselves of discriminatory attitudes, despite having a democratic responsibility to all those they represent – including people with mental health problems.

Finally, many witnesses pointed to the paucity of knowledge and research in the area of social exclusion and mental health. There have been attempts recently to quantify social exclusion, for example by the New Policy Institute/Joseph Rowntree Foundation (Howarth *et al.* 1998), but the specific patterns of exclusion experienced by mental health service users are not yet well understood:

Our current understanding of the exclusion and marginalisation process is not particularly strong. If we wish to break the cycle of social exclusion for [people with mental health problems] we need to identify the risk factors for becoming marginalised and the protective factors that prevent marginalisation or aid reintegration. Studies need to address the reasons for disengagement and the pathways back to inclusion (Sainsbury Centre for Mental Health 1998).

1.3 **Summary and conclusions**

The Panel received strong and consistent evidence of the discrimination people experience as a direct result of their mental health problems. This discrimination, which occurs in every facet of life, combines to make mental health service users vulnerable to extreme social exclusion. The processes of social exclusion further exacerbate mental health problems, and the treatment and support services currently offered to service users can increase rather than decrease social exclusion.

Mental health and social exclusion – the problems
Employment
- The justified fear of experiencing discrimination at work prevents many users of mental health services from applying for work, and from disclosing their mental health problems once in work.
- There are many openly discriminatory practices at work pertaining to mental health problems, as exemplified by a general practitioner's contract that allowed his colleagues to sack him if he were to be sectioned under the Mental Health Act.
- Many employers feel under-informed and under-prepared for dealing with mental health problems in the workplace.
- Careful guidelines for employers about disclosure and confidentiality are needed. Currently many service users are justifiably unwilling to disclose their mental health problems for fear this will be used against them. Equally, employers need to be aware of support needs.
- The Disability Discrimination Act lacks proper enforcement mechanisms, and is seen by many employers as relating only to physical or sensory impairments. There is little understanding of what might constitute 'reasonable adjustments' under the Disability Discrimination Act in relation to mental health problems.
- Mental health services – in both clinical and social support settings – do not see promoting work for service users as part of their role.
- Even when the mental health services themselves are the employer, there is a powerful and pervasive assumption that having a diagnosis of mental ill-health inevitably means you are 'not up to the job'.
- Employment within the mainstream – with support where needed – must be the aim, rather than segregated work schemes that maintain the 'them and us' divide between service users and the rest of the community.

- Employment and support must be tailored to individual needs. It is important the service users are not 'set up to fail', thus further damaging self-esteem.
- While employment initiatives are sorely needed within mental health, policy-makers and providers must not see ability to work as the only measure of a person's worth. Everyone has the right to be included, regardless of their ability to make an 'economic contribution'.
- The previous point is particularly relevant to services for young people. There are times when young people do not have the resources to work, and times when work will be detrimental to mental health.
- There are a number of benefit disincentives to work, which need urgent reform if they are not to continue to promote social exclusion for people using mental health services.
- There is no central, national body promoting employment for mental health service users.

Education and training

- There is little knowledge or understanding of mental health issues in many schools, colleges or universities. Educational bodies do not know where to go for advice and guidance, due in part to the lack of a central body specifically promoting access to education for students with mental health problems.
- Provision for disabled access by the higher education funding councils is very piecemeal because it is dependent on the optional co-operation of individual institutions.
- The Disability Discrimination Act does not cover education, and discriminatory practice that would be illegal in employment is still pervasive and unchallenged within education. Within further and higher education students are routinely rejected at application stage on the basis that they have had mental health problems.
- Segregated teaching – most particularly in schools – is still happening, and the current trend of school exclusions will only add to this problem.
- Practical support mechanisms for people with mental health problems, relating for example to benefits, transport and on-campus support, are almost non-existent within further and higher education.
- The structure of many courses – for example the necessity to complete within limited time-frames – can discriminate against people with mental health problems, who may experience their problems episodically but be prevented after recovery from picking up where they left off. Current benefits arrangements also make flexibility very difficult.
- Mental health support work within education needs to continue to address

issues such as suicide and self-harm which are receiving some attention, but should also look particularly at the mental health needs of mature students, part-time students, international students and minority ethnic students.

- Problems within education are compounded by the failure of different authorities and agencies involved in provision to work together to ensure services are delivered. Mental health services have been very slow to link up with education authorities and agencies to promote equality of opportunity for people with mental health problems, despite attention being drawn to the issue in recent official education reviews such as the Tomlinson report *Inclusive Learning* (1996).

Access to goods, services and social networks

- The discrimination and exclusion experienced by people who use mental health services were felt to be triggered by the diagnosis of mental health problems and the subsequent treatments, not to be a result of the mental health problems themselves.
- Many users feel that a psychiatric diagnosis has made them non-citizens, with no rights, no credibility and no redress.
- The ostracisation of mental health service users leads to difficulties in establishing social networks, a lack of informal job contacts, and a lack of access to everyday goods and services:
  - Lack of access to banking services is a common problem for mental health service users, and a key determinant in social exclusion.
  - Insurance services for people with mental health problems are an ongoing problem needing further research and a critical look at how actuarial data is arrived at and used in relation to mental ill-health.
- The media has tremendous power in creating and perpetuating discriminatory attitudes towards mental health service users. The voice of service users themselves is almost absent from mainstream media.
- People from minority ethnic groups who also experience mental health problems are more than doubly excluded. Racist discrimination has a material impact on mental health.
- Families and carers can be affected by the discrimination experienced by people with mental health problems, which can lead to ruptured family networks, and to exclusion of carers and relatives by the wider community.
- Experiencing mental health problems and the subsequent loss of family and social support networks can lead to housing problems, including homelessness. Equally, poor housing or homelessness contributes greatly to mental distress.

Mental health services

- Instead of leading to a therapeutic or supporting process, a psychiatric diagnosis can be the start of a process of social exclusion. This process is triggered in part by the nature of psychiatric services themselves, which are experienced as ghettoised and stigmatising.

- Some service users are in active flight from psychiatric services, which they consider have not only failed to address their needs, but have contributed to their problems.

- The symptoms of adverse side-effects of some psychiatric medications, for example tardive dyskinesia [see Glossary] caused by neuroleptic medication [see Glossary], are in themselves a cause of discriminatory behaviour by an ill-informed public.

- Mental health services focus on the medical or clinical to the detriment of the social. Clinicians and community support workers must understand mental health problems in relation to the disabling effects of discrimination.

- The absence of this understanding impacts particularly badly on service users from minority ethnic groups, lesbian and gay service users, or those who have physical or sensory impairments. It also makes services for people with a 'dual diagnosis' (see Glossary) particularly fragmented, inadequate and conflicted.

- Where culturally appropriate services have been established – often within the voluntary sector by members of a particular community – statutory services have a tendency to see that as a justification for withdrawing support, rather than as an opportunity to work in an integrated manner with other services in order to improve statutory provision.

- The National Health Service, despite ideals of equal access enshrined in policy, engages in discriminatory and excluding behaviour towards people with mental health problems, who may find themselves struck off GP's lists, or receiving inadequate secondary or tertiary general health care.

- Services for adolescents (14–25 year olds) are an area of particular concern. There is a gap between current child and adolescent mental health services and adult mental health services which is causing a great deal of unnecessary distress to already vulnerable young people.

- Nimby campaigns continue to disrupt the provision of community mental health facilities. Local politicians and other elected officials, who have a community leadership role and a responsibility to ensure that people already subject to discrimination are not further excluded, often do not shoulder responsibility for tackling nimbyism, tending instead to fuel it by focusing on containment and risk issues.

• Mental health services have been slow to take on the entire issue of social exclusion. There is almost no specific research about mental health and social exclusion, and very little acknowledgement that promoting inclusion needs to become integral to the aims of good mental health policy and care.

Conclusions

The evidence was powerful testament to the 'holistic' nature of social exclusion – both cause and effect are multi-faceted and interconnected. Figure 1 (p. 46) gives a broad schematic outline of the issues uncovered. As the figure illustrates, outcomes are interconnected in complex ways. In addition, all the connecting lines in the figure are two-way, so that a simple 'cause and effect' model cannot be applied. The experience of mental health service users also gives the lie to theories that social exclusion is 'another way of describing poverty'. Mental health problems, it is clear, can be both a cause and result of low income, but it is also clear that mental ill-health can be unrelated to poverty, and that mechanisms of exclusion triggered by it come into play irrespective of income. In this regard also the Inquiry findings reiterate and confirm existing research. They make clear that a definition of social exclusion that focuses solely on employment and the labour market is misplaced and partial, and that, equally, any attempt to address mental health problems that does not take into account the material circumstances of service users will be critically undermined.

Crucially, the Inquiry evidence regarding the experiences of discrimination makes it very clear that the improvement of material resources – for example by increasing welfare provision and 'skilling-up' – would not eliminate the problems of exclusion on its own. As the evidence makes clear, providing people with mental health problems with a basic standard of living and the skills to compete in the job market is crucial. But equally crucial are challenges to the excluding nature of institutions and individuals within society – i.e. promoting what has been termed social cohesion (Miller 1999). The evidence to the Inquiry detailed excluding behaviour by organisations across the public, private and voluntary sector, and also by mental health services themselves. Miller (1999) has noted the importance of recognising that promoting inclusion is the responsibility of all sectors of society:

> In discussions about promoting social cohesion, people often use the term management to mean 'public sector management'. Public services do contribute a large share towards supporting practices that promote social cohesion, but we need a broader definition. The private and voluntary sectors are also involved, both as contractors to the public sector and as providers of jobs, goods and services that are part of the life-blood of civil

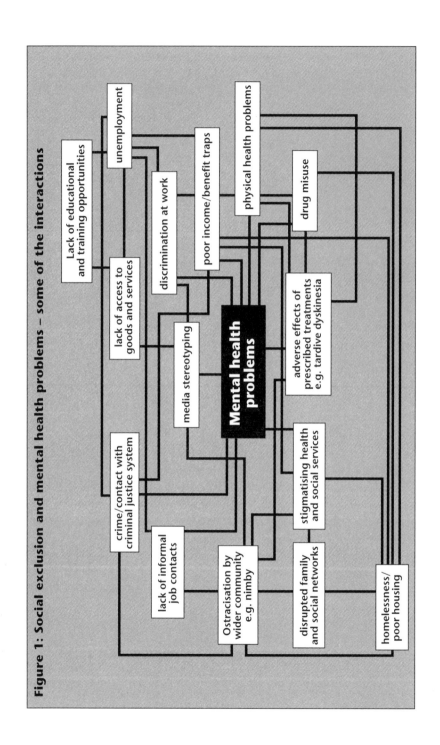

Figure 1: Social exclusion and mental health problems – some of the interactions

Lack of educational and training opportunities

unemployment

discrimination at work

poor income/benefit traps

physical health problems

drug misuse

lack of access to goods and services

media stereotyping

Mental health problems

adverse effects of prescribed treatments e.g. tardive dyskinesia

crime/contact with criminal justice system

stigmatising health and social services

lack of informal job contacts

Ostracisation by wider community e.g. nimby

disrupted family and social networks

homelessness/ poor housing

CREATING ACCEPTING COMMUNITIES

society. Intentionally and unintentionally as spin-offs, private sector activities can promote or undermine social cohesion. The public – as individuals, households and communities – also contribute to social cohesion through their day-to-day interactions and life choices.

When it comes to mental health problems, the excluding behaviours of both institutions and individuals are pervasive, and often allied to fear and ignorance. They need tackling with both education and legislation, and also with concerted and strategic use of the media.

The evidence, and the process of gathering it, also threw up important concerns about how to gauge social exclusion. It is quite clear that traditional models used to measure poverty, which took an arbitrary 'poverty line' and used income measurements to see who fell above and below it, are entirely inadequate in the face of the matrix of cause and effect uncovered in relation to mental health and social exclusion. The authors of a recent groundbreaking attempt to monitor social exclusion by the Joseph Rowntree Foundation/New Policy Institute (Howarth *et al.* 1998) noted significant gaps in currently available official data in areas concerning children, young adults, mental health and people with disabilities – all areas particularly pertinent to this Inquiry (Street 1999).

The process of inviting evidence and taking oral and written submissions direct from individuals experiencing or attempting to counter exclusion was seen as an important corrective to the sometimes removed and sterile quantitative research methods that drive health and social policy. There is a great need for the people who are excluded to get a chance to define what exclusion is – otherwise the debates about its nature and solutions run the risk of becoming exclusionary themselves. Qualitative data – direct experiential information about what happens to people and how it makes them feel – tells us much that we cannot otherwise know about how multiple discriminations overlap, and how exclusion builds up over time and across different facets of people's lives.

Obtaining evidence in this way also recognises that the experts in how to counter social exclusion are the people experiencing it. The increasing acknowledgement by the Government that 'joined-up problems require joined-up solutions' is welcomed by everyone wanting to see a happier and healthier society. But unless policy-makers begin to recognise the importance of the contribution of 'experts by experience', to both research processes and resulting strategic planning, policy changes will remain just that – changes to policy that do not change people's lives.

CHAPTER 2

'The value of a person, the value of a community':

ethics and social inclusion

2.1 **What is a community?**

Any discussion about social exclusion will involve ethical stances, whether explicit or not. In order to develop a coherent view of how social exclusion operates in relation to people with mental health problems, it is necessary to tease out some of the common assumptions about 'community', individuals and the state that might underpin mental health policy and wider social policy.

Miller (1999) created a set of 'models of community' which sheds useful light on how an agenda for social inclusion for people with mental health problems might be formed. He defines four models of 'ideal' communities: exclusive diversity, inclusive diversity, required inclusion and voluntary inclusion. The 'exclusive diversity' model is a community made up of a diverse range of socially exclusive groups. In this fragmented community, exclusion is seen as inevitable unless individuals help themselves. Intervention by the state is seen as undermining, as reinforcing a 'victim' culture. The way forward is for people to build their own positive self-image within groups of their own choice, and so adherents to this model are primarily concerned with advocating self-help approaches to tackle exclusion. This model underpins some radical grassroots community movements, faith communities, and radical groups of people with disabilities, including mental health problems.

The second model, 'inclusive diversity', also sees society as diverse rather than homogeneous. The key difference is that it interprets the promotion of inclusion as actively fostering the interdependence between people and between diverse groups. It recognises that some members of the community will be able to pursue their preferred lifestyles, but that others may lack the resources to do so and need help, both from other groups and from the state. It also recognises that diversity can lead one group to discriminate against another, and that the state needs to intervene both to foster diversity and to arbitrate over conflicts.

'Required inclusion' takes a rather different view of what society is. In this model, the ideal community is homogeneous, with a single set of norms and values to which everyone should wish to adhere. In this model the state not only provides opportunities for inclusion, but also articulates the moral code of the community and ensures that all institutions conform. (Some critics of 'assertive outreach' policies in mental health have interpreted such policies as a form of required inclusion.) In this model, social exclusion is tackled by state policies that make opportunities available to all those who adhere to the values of the state. It also promotes policies that limit the impact of the excluded upon the included.

Finally, 'voluntary inclusion' also takes as its starting-point the desirability of a homogeneous state to which everyone should aspire to be a part. This model differs from required inclusion in that groups or individuals that become detached from the mainstream are assumed to do so because of their own social deficits such as lack of skills. The responsibility to effect their own inclusion therefore lies primarily with the groups or individuals themselves, rather than a coercive state. The state must make sure that services are available to all, but must not provide services specific to these groups as this will promote dependency.

The excluding community

Why do people with mental health problems experience social exclusion? Partly this may result from their experience of communities and the ways in which they work. Whatever form communities take, prevailing attitudes to mental ill-health and disability within them have not been based, to date, on any ideas of common interest or identity. Rather, these have strongly reinforced notions of difference – and inferiority. From a psychological standpoint, it has been argued that communities have 'a vested interest in "warehousing" those people who are identified as being mad, bad, or useless, if only in order that those who remain at large can safely project all their mad, bad and useless bits into them, disowning them in themselves' (Foster and Roberts 1999). This has profound implications for our understanding of how to tackle social exclusion in mental health.

2.2 **Evidence presented to the Inquiry**

Submissions to the Inquiry concerning ethics and social exclusion all focused, from different angles, on the relationship between the individual and society, the interplay between rights and responsibilities, and the ways in which members of society value each other.

The value of a person

Every piece of evidence submitted to the Inquiry, in one form or another, was grounded on the need to recognise the absolute and equal value of every individual. Much of the evidence concerning the experience of social exclusion detailed in section 1.2 (p. 11) shows that once a label of mental illness has been attached to an individual, it has the effect implicitly, and often explicitly, of devaluing them. Some witnesses explored the possible reasons behind this:

> What does equality actually mean? I would say dignity in value, respect, and an equal right to be taken seriously in our own terms, to be respected for who we are, for our experiences and our beliefs. This is actually very challenging, because there is an instinctive human response to create norms of behaviour in society. The moment you start talking about mental illness you are setting up a norm and deviance from the norm. In our current society three things flow from the term 'mental illness': if I am ill then my ability to play a part in society is impaired until I am well; if I am ill then out of compassion you have a human obligation to help me get well; and if I resist your attempts to make me well then either I lack capacity or I am choosing to be ill and therefore 'bad'.
>
> In order to give true equality of dignity, value and respect to an individual we must as a society accept that attitudes and experiences that seem bizarre and baffling and frightening are still within the range of what is meant by being a human being and a member of society. *Simon Foster, Mind*

> To my mind the biggest problem we have to overcome is society's psychological exclusion of people who they see as different from themselves. We all have within ourselves impulses we cannot accept, for unbridled violence, or unbridled sexuality – many of the religions of the world focus on how to control these impulses. But

the fact that we cannot accept these things in ourselves, this process of denial, leads us to project these terrible things onto others who seemingly don't belong to us, whom we cannot acknowledge as being part of our society and whom we therefore do not need to value. *Julian Leff, Institute of Psychiatry*

The question of how people are and should be valued threw up some fundamental questions about, amongst other things, economics and work. Many witnesses felt that the ability to work should not be the only test of someone's value:

We live in a society that has a central notion about making an economic contribution. In simple terms this means that you can only take part in society if you bring something with you. The effect of this is twofold: it is not enough to bring yourself, so that is a devaluation of the person; and you can only take rather than give for a limited period of time. So the person who has little or nothing to offer in economic terms becomes excluded because they cannot make a contribution. *Arthur Hawes, Archdeacon of Lincoln*

We know that the outcome of the severely mentally ill is at least twice as good in the economically developing world as it is in the west. We don't know exactly why this is, but one reason may be that they are not operating in such thoroughly industrialised societies where competitiveness, timekeeping and productivity are the key aims. Family organisations and enterprises can be very tolerant of people's disabilities. It is possible for people who are quite disabled by mental illness in developing countries to contribute, to feel they are part of a family endeavour for creating wealth, and are not excluded as they are in western capitalist society. *Julian Leff, Institute of Psychiatry*

It's very difficult to see how people can be given equal value in a culture of competition. I think we have to turn the whole thing on its head and actually realise that what a disabled person or someone with mental health problems brings to society *is their disability,* and the challenge that brings to society. Because when we decide to look for solutions to these problems, instead of excluding them, then we all move forward and our attitudes towards people's value and rights are fundamentally changed. *Micheline Mason, Alliance for Inclusive Education*

In relation to diversity, if you are able to express a view then that view contributes to the wealth of ideas that a collective has. And beyond that is your ability to contribute to wealth, but for me not wealth as in pounds, shillings and pence but wealth as in wellbeing. There are a great number of unidentified resources in our communities, so that what appears to be a cost can be turned around to be a benefit. *Perry Walker, New Economics Foundation*

Also highlighted was the need to avoid simplistic definitions of what 'productivity' actually is:

The idea that many disabled people don't work has never actually been true, they have always worked very hard within the institutions in which they have been put – but they were never actually paid. The money was put into their so-called care. *Micheline Mason, Alliance for Inclusive Education*

Many people will be familiar with the idea of LETS [local exchange trading systems – see Glossary]. As just one example, a group of people in Warminster with mental health difficulties set themselves up as a LETS team [see p. 75]. Not all of them were able to work every day, but as a team they could commit to a job and carry it out. So what did they get out of it? First, they felt valued, somebody was prepared to pay them for what they could do. Second, they were doing it collectively and gained a sense of companionship. Third, what they earned on the LETS enabled them to get things they otherwise couldn't afford, for example massages at the local mental health day centre. So, LETS schemes have ethical messages contained within them: 'I am valued', 'We live by our values', 'We are creating our own money'. It is a lot more effective than giving a lecture about the democratisation of money. It's a system, a tool, which contains a whole different set of ethics within it. *Perry Walker, New Economics Foundation*

I think the idea of LETS schemes and other forms of social firm [see

Glossary] is a vital ingredient in thinking about inclusion for people with mental health problems. We need to promote co-operative endeavours run with equal power by professionals and service users, so together they create a system that brings users into contact with 'the public' in an ordinary, healthy transaction. The processes we need in place to effect this would be very difficult in open employment, but can be done through the creation and support of these innovative schemes. *Julian Leff, Institute of Psychiatry*

Am I 'my brother's keeper'?

Some witnesses felt that the consequences of distorted value systems, of seeing people only as economic benefits or deficits, contributed to an erosion of the concept of mutual support within communities:

> The churches and the great world religions provide an alternative understanding to the notion of people equating to an economic factor, because they start with a different doctrine of being human. The doctrine derived from religious faith understands human beings as created in the image of God. That means they are created as good, fallen, capable of redemption, and as individuals in their own right. In the Christian faith the doctrine of the creator includes the fatherhood of God and from this derives the brotherhood of man. In Pauline theology the church is understood as one body in which people are mutually responsible. The net result of such a system is that 'I *am* my brother's keeper'. This leads to the conclusion that the churches, because of their very nature, have the responsibility to create, develop and sustain community life where people can be treated as individuals, included and mutually supported. *Arthur Hawes, Archdeacon of Lincoln*

> The Jewish community has always prided itself on its ability to look after its own. I think this stems from biblical precepts, where 10 per cent of the fields were left fallow for farming by people who could not afford to have their own land. This is translated into the notion that 10 per cent of one's income should be donated to charity. *Simon Morris, Jewish Care*

Such theological concepts themselves contain areas of conflict and tension, however, which are paralleled in people's daily lives:

In Christian theology there is a conflict between being made in the image of God and also being part of the body. These two images run side-by-side and sometimes seem to conflict. The parallel here is that the needs, desires and rights of the individual living in society may also conflict with the wider community. *Arthur Hawes, Archdeacon of Lincoln*

Possible conflict between concepts of autonomy and care in specific relation to mental ill-health could come in a variety of forms. For example, an individual's right to determine their own life may result in actions or outcomes that others consider not to be in the person's best interests:

If I have a mental health problem, and you, out of care for my wellbeing, want to intervene, then I have an absolute right to choose whether or not I accept this intervention. This is a very difficult area. If I am in distress, and harming myself, and I refuse your attempts to help me, are you entitled to intervene against my wishes? I would say no. If I am capable of making a choice then you do not have the right to override that choice.

If I am not capable of making a choice, and I have given no previous pointers as to my wishes, for example in an advance directive, then the only test is surely what you would choose if you were in my position. I use those words carefully, rather than 'what is in my best interests', because that phrase objectifies me. What you would choose if you were me and what you consider to be in my best interests might be different. *Simon Foster, Mind*

A culture operating on the basis of paternalism rather than participation may think it is offering care and support, but may not be meeting real needs:

I think the down side of some voluntary care organisations is that we can provide care in a very paternalistic way. We can be patriarchal, hierarchical, with the effect that the managers and those involved in the giving of money do so in a benevolent manner. There is a tendency to perceive a need and then decide upon the response, rather than involve users and listen to what users want. *Simon Morris, Jewish Care*

The culture of paternalism, and the imbalances of power that give rise to it, will also determine who is prioritised for treatment, and what treatment they receive in what circumstances.

In English Common Law the principle of personal autonomy finds expression in the protection of a person from any medical intervention or treatment to which they have not consented. This principle of autonomy is most often ethically problematic in the field of mental health as it appears to be compromised each time someone is detained in hospital under the Mental Health Act, or required to be subject to supervision in the community.

One of the justifications for this is the 'right to receive treatment'. Decisions are taken by others for the person to be given treatment, if they are deemed to lack the capacity to make a judgement for themselves. This looks neat in theory but is highly problematic. Who defines capacity and how? If incapacity is equated with a person 'lacking insight', this may mean only that the person disagrees with what is proposed for them. There remain great imbalances of power in therapeutic relationships, which must be acknowledged and countered if this argument is to work fairly in practice.

The second justification is the 'rescue' argument. This is not triggered by the assumption of incapacity, but is justified in order to prevent a person from harming themselves. Some people forcefully argue that this justification should not be available if a person has previously and reliably declared their unwillingness to be 'rescued' in this way. *Ian Bynoe, formerly Mind (written evidence)*

Some witnesses pointed out that within the legal and clinical framework, questions of resources, and policy-driven motives, will also profoundly affect how care is apportioned:

The suicide rate is now a [Health of the Nation – see Glossary] indicator of success for mental health service providers; I need to be able to prove that the suicide rate in my area is going down. One group of people at risk of suicide is those with severe mental illness. The consequence of being set targets is to try and identify suicide risks and give them priority over non-suicide risks. I don't know if this is ethical, but I do know it's a result of the targets. *Lionel Joyce, Newcastle NHS Trust*

Badness and illness

Many witnesses to the Inquiry were concerned about the association between violent behaviour and mental ill-health. The point has been made in Chapter 1 (p. 8) about ill-informed media presenting all people with mental health problems as potential violent criminals. Some witnesses also pointed to the ways in which Government policy and also clinical practice can reinforce this link:

> I have been thinking for some time about the issue of people diagnosed with severe antisocial personality disorder who commit heinous crimes. I can understand how the psychiatric services first became involved with these people – because there was nowhere else for them to go, because they often have the most horrendous backgrounds and invite compassion and sympathy, and because a percentage of them may be helped by good psychological treatment. However, as a result of a process of 'guilt by association', people with bipolar disorder, schizophrenia and depression are being threatened with compulsory treatments and compulsory detention completely inappropriately. I have weighed all the arguments, and I feel it is in the overwhelming interests of the majority of people with severe mental illness that I label people diagnosed with severe personality disorder who commit these crimes as bad. They belong in the prison system or some other system associated with that group and should no longer be allowed to be labelled severely mentally ill. *Lionel Joyce, Newcastle NHS Trust*

> I think we are in danger of losing the possibility that people can do things because they are selfish, greedy or envious. I think morality is being clinicalised, and we have to make a plea for the place of personal choice. So I think we actually should treat people slightly differently: if somebody is bad theologically you seek to redeem them, if they are ill you seek to care for them. *Arthur Hawes, Archdeacon of Lincoln*

> If I am behaving in a harmful or dangerous way then you have every right to stop me, and to enlist society's help in stopping me. However, this is to do with my *behaviour*, and is nothing to do with a psychiatric diagnosis. We must treat people equally on the basis of their behaviour, not of diagnosis. In addition, if you regard my

behaviour as being so unacceptable that you justify detaining me, that does not automatically mean that you are entitled to treat me. In the first place, clinicians will attest that it is very difficult to determine whether treating a particular person will reduce the risk they pose. In the second place, I still have the right to make a choice about treatment, so I have the right to say that I do not want treatment, even if the clinician says that such treatment will reduce my dangerousness and enable me to re-enter society. I have the right to say that I would rather be confined than accept this as the price for my liberty. *Simon Foster, Mind*

I can think of two cases recently where we had a full homicide inquiry. One of our long-term patients, diagnosed with schizophrenia, killed his mother, after having been to the outpatient clinic and declined medication. It was the view of the medical team who had known him for a number of years that what he did was commit murder. He hated his mother, had done for years, and he murdered her. The psychiatrist who interviewed him shortly afterwards felt there was no element of psychosis, and the murder was a calculated event. But the Crown Prosecution Service and the courts found it, I suspect, convenient – and society is happy to collude in this as well – to decide that he had committed the murder because of his illness. He would get an order under the Mental Health Act, would get effective treatment because he is not that ill and would be discharged quite quickly.

In the other case, a woman who had stabbed and killed her baby was subsequently interviewed by a psychiatrist, who felt there was no mental illness present. But again the reaction of society was that she must be mentally ill, the judgement of the psychiatrist was set aside, and the person concerned is still receiving psychiatric treatment. We have to ask ourselves what is going on with these decisions. Are we allowing ourselves to be corrupted? I feel there is something very corrupt about these series of judgements that I feel deeply unhappy about. *Lionel Joyce, Newcastle NHS Trust*

Risk and rehabilitation
The notion of risk looms large in much mental health discourse, though it is often interpreted in a narrow way – usually either in terms of the risk of harm to the public judged to be posed by people with mental health

problems, or the risk of harm to themselves. Witnesses drew attention to the need to think realistically about levels of risk and to balance them against possible benefits:

> We are in the business of risk-taking. If we do not take risks we cannot treat people. You cannot be rehabilitated if you are on a locked ward, if you are not exposed to society, if you are not given the chance to walk down the street and live in normal housing. *Lionel Joyce, Newcastle NHS Trust*

> If you want people to heal you've got to take risks. It's well documented in general surgery that if you've got a ward with elderly people with mobility problems is it better that they try to remain mobile and run the risk of falling and breaking a hip, because the alternative is to become immobile. *Arthur Hawes, Archdeacon of Lincoln*

> The 'third-party harm' argument within current legislation provides the justification for detaining a person reckoned to pose a risk of harm to another. It is central to our common law, to statutory mental health legislation, and to the empowering of courts to detain those found guilty of criminal offences. The existence and use of this justification to remove and exclude people has helped to perpetuate the myth that anyone requiring treatment for mental health problems must constitute a public danger; it must be regarded as part of the problem of social exclusion. It helps to create public acceptance for the argument of Dr Deahl, a consultant psychiatrist working in east London, that he would prefer to detain nine patients unfairly than have one commit violence in the community. *Ian Bynoe, formerly Mind (written evidence)*

Other witnesses pointed out that the evaluation of risks involved in mental health care and rehabilitation must not be driven by dogma on either side. While risk evaluations should not be discriminatory and lead to defensive outcomes, neither should they over-estimate the capabilities or under-estimate the needs of the individuals concerned. Risk must be understood in terms of the pressures that individuals are subjected to if care and treatment are inappropriately withdrawn:

We recognise some rehabilitative value in the absence of deterioration. We have developed a notion of a 'staircase with many landings' as a helpful way to articulate our experience, which is that rehabilitation is not necessarily incremental or linear. We believe strongly that goals for personal development and rehabilitation have to be realistic. Some people require considerable support – allied to significant personal effort – in order simply to stand still. 'Containment' is an unfashionable sentiment because it is held to correlate with notions of high security and public threat. At its best, however, it is concerned with not placing burdens of expectation on people who are ill-equipped to realise them. *Charles Fraser, St Mungo's*

Participation and empowerment

One of the key concepts for many witnesses was participation – possibly the vital antidote to social exclusion. Witnesses stressed at the outset two fundamental rights to democratic participation currently explicitly denied to people with mental health problems: the right to vote and the right to serve on a jury. People detained in hospital under the Mental Health Act are entitled to vote as long as they are on the electoral register. (They are subject to the capacity test applied to all electors.) However, under the Representation of the People Act 1983 patients cannot use the hospital address as their residence on the register. Special, but unsatisfactory, arrangements exist to allow voluntary patients to register at any previous address. Even these unsatisfactory arrangements do not, however, apply to detained patients, many of whom therefore become disenfranchised. The relevant Home Office Circular (RPA 407) suggests that doubts will arise over anyone who has severed the link with their previous address or has been away from their home for more than six months.

Under the Juries Act 1974 'mentally disordered persons' are ineligible to serve on a jury. The definition of a mentally disordered person is very wide – it includes those who are justifiably excluded because of their incapacity but could also encompass those taking antidepressant medication for example, or attending quarterly appointments with a psychiatrist.

While these two examples might be seen as anomalous, they do reflect underlying assumptions about who should have the right to participate in civil society. Overturning these sometimes buried assumptions on the part of society in general is a complex task:

I think there is a move towards inclusion, but very few people understand what it actually means. I think it's to do with empowering people who need help. Learning to support people without disempowering them is the key. Losing control of your life is what drives people crazy and makes them do terrible things. We must empower people to make decisions for themselves, to learn about the consequences of making them, that way we can allow people to make the contribution they can make. *Micheline Mason, Alliance for Inclusive Education*

The principle of the right to participate is closely allied to the concept of equal opportunity. The reasons why people with mental health problems find participation difficult should determine the responses the community makes. Factors involving gender or ethnicity may contribute to these barriers to participation, and must be addressed if the right to participate is to be genuinely upheld.

Possible responses cover a vast spectrum. They would include social security measures that maintain the personal means of those unable to support themselves, recognising the extra costs of long-term illness and disability. Employers and those providing consumer services and facilities may be required to adapt their workplace, procedures or practices. Patient advocacy services in hospitals and communities can be encouraged to provide a voice for those using services.

Cost and the overall distribution of resources may be factors that set limits on the right to participation; but the overall distribution of resources must be searchingly examined if traditional and discriminatory patterns are not to be perpetuated. In some instances costs would fall on private individuals or organisations, in others they would be collectively borne, by taxpayers for example. For all its flaws, the way in which an employer's duty to make 'reasonable adjustments' is framed in the Disability Discrimination Act 1995 illustrates how the scope of an obligation can be limited in practice, though in a flexible way, to ensure that some fairness is preserved. *Ian Bynoe, formerly Mind (written evidence)*

Getting people to participate in planning processes, whether of health and social services or local environmental issues, is another determinant in the process of inclusion:

> We all have the right to participate in planning our own lives. One of the keys to realising this is to bring together all the stakeholders. The jargon is 'whole system events' [see Glossary]; if you really involve all the people who need to be involved then the chances are much higher you will get a workable solution. I heard a story of a whole system event in Newcastle where a woman told of the awful experience her husband had had when being discharged from hospital. She and a group of friends then got together to think of another name for hospital discharge. They came back and said they would like to call it 'going home'. Now I can see it may not apply if you are going to a hostel, but nonetheless it is a good deal friendlier than the alternative the professionals came up with – 'readmission to the community'. That's a simple example of what happens when you let people into their own lives. *Perry Walker, New Economics Foundation*

The notion of participation is not just a two-way street, but a whole confluence, a conjunction of all the interested parties. So within mental health services, for example, the participation of relatives needs to be integral to the process, so that the notion of participation does not hang solely on the user-provider axis:

> Relatives of people with mental health problems can become very isolated. The NHS needs to establish relatives' groups – they are really not good at involving relatives. Voluntary organisations like the National Schizophrenia Fellowship have been doing this for years, but the NHS has hardly any relatives' groups; they empower relatives, which is vital. *Julian Leff, Institute of Psychiatry*

Opting out, and the reciprocity principle

While the right of participation was a universally supported goal, some witnesses were concerned that what must be promoted as a right should not be transformed into a duty, and pointed clearly to the need to recognise a right *not* to participate:

I get a bit wary about the word 'community'. We've heard an awful lot about communities and the right to participate, but we must remember that the very idea of a community is exclusive by definition, and I would like to defend the right not to participate and not to be punished or have your rights to services revoked because of that. *Charles Fraser, St Mungo's*

And another warning note about currently stylish notions of 'reciprocity' was also sounded:

In mental health policy, and law particularly, the latest notion is the 'reciprocity principle'. This asserts that detention and other restrictions can be justified as long as they are balanced by reciprocal obligations imposed on the state; for example to provide high quality services responsive to the needs of service users. However, there is a danger that reciprocity will be turned from a principle emphasising the responsibility of the community into one stressing obligations on the part of the individual, for example to accept restrictions as a precondition for receiving services. One US state now requires service recipients to receive their medication before they are allowed to collect their social security entitlement. It would be disastrous for the UK to go down this route. *Ian Bynoe, formerly Mind (written evidence)*

2.3 **Summary and conclusions**

The evidence given to the Panel covered a range of the ethical issues underlying the problem of the exclusion of people with mental health problems. There was agreement about the basic need to recognise the absolute value of the individual. Witnesses varied, however, in their perceptions of the community as a potentially supportive or potentially coercive or oppressive influence on the individual.

Ethics in mental health – the issues
- The ethical bedrock of any challenge to the social exclusion of people with mental health problems is the recognition of the absolute value of the individual human being.

- Attitudes and experiences that seem bizarre and baffling are still within the range of what it means to be human, and therefore to be valued. This point is particularly relevant in circumstances where what are normal attitudes, behaviours or experiences in non-western cultures can be wrongly construed as pathological by the dominant western culture.
- Notions of human value in contemporary society are confused and debased by economic values.
- The promotion of inclusion needs to involve imaginative approaches to traditional concepts of work and money, including, for example, the democratisation of work through social firms (see Glossary), and the democratisation of money through LETS schemes (see Glossary).
- As every individual has an absolute value, so every individual has a right to self-determination. A paternalistic therapeutic culture, while it may feel it is fulfilling duties of care and responsibility for its members, may disregard or obliterate self-determination.
- Questions of defining capacity need to be searchingly examined if they are not to replicate existing inequalities within therapeutic relationships.
- There is a danger that morality is being 'clinicalised'. The drive to label all people who commit crimes as 'ill' has a highly stigmatising effect on those diagnosed as 'ill' who do not commit any crime.
- A realistic understanding of risk is sorely needed. This will involve a holistic view of risk, a broader understanding of harm, and looking at potential harm done *to* mental health service users, not just by them. It will also involve an acceptance by society that all rehabilitation – all progress – involves risk.
- In order to promote social inclusion, and ultimately social cohesion (see p. 46), the recognition of the value of the individual must be twinned with the recognition of the individual's right to participate. Mechanisms preventing participation, which include poverty and discrimination, must be challenged, and new ways of incorporating people into the democratic and bureaucratic processes that shape their lives must be championed.

Conclusions

The concept of social exclusion brings into question fundamental moral and ethical assumptions. It is vital that these assumptions are made explicit and debated, as they will drive the policy agenda currently being created to tackle exclusion.

Several witnesses to the Inquiry warned of the danger of assuming that there is some ideal homogeneous community of which everyone wants to be a part. The consensus of the evidence the Panel heard outlined a society based on the idea of 'inclusive diversity'. As Miller (1999) has outlined, this is a model of society that 'recognises that social homogeneity is more apparent than real, and diversity a feature of all parts of all communities rather than that of specific groups. It views inclusion as the interdependence of people and wishes to exploit the potential to be gained by people working together. However, it does not assume that this will always occur naturally but believes it must be continuously fostered.'

The recognition of difference, and indeed the valuing of difference, is therefore crucial. However, in recognising that society is not homogeneous, it is equally important not to fall into the assumption that fragmentation is therefore inevitable or desirable. A constant thread of the Inquiry evidence was the danger of ghettoising. A model of society that accepts that fragmentation is inevitable might regard the supporting of excluded groups in forming their own communities as a laudable aim. But witnesses to the Inquiry were united in their opposition to this position. One witness summed it up thus: 'Putting "types" of people together in institutions and pretending an equally valid community has been formed does not work. They just get to be meaningless together.' (Micheline Mason, see p. 28).

In effect, the evidence revealed the necessity of a constant 'balancing act' between recognising difference while according equal treatment, countering fragmentation while supporting diversity. It made it very clear that any ethical approach to mental health must be capable of recognising *both* the importance of our social embeddedness *and* of respect for the individual. The process of promoting social inclusion of people with mental health problems, by its very nature, can only take place in a context that recognises the importance of social forces within communities, and in order to do this it must take the concerns of all stakeholders seriously. Ultimately, mental health is a resource that benefits individuals, but can only be developed in relation to others.

Finally, implicit in this recognition of inclusive diversity is acknowledgement that tackling the exclusion of people with mental health problems has benefits for the rest of 'the community'. These benefits are found in an increase in what has been termed social capital (Wilkinson 1996) – qualities of trust and tolerance, levels of civic engagement and association. As we will see in the next chapter, witnesses argue convincingly that practical measures to include people with mental health problems will also benefit others.

CHAPTER 3

'Coming in from the cold':

promoting social inclusion for people with mental health problems

3.1 Existing research and good practice

There is already much work being done in the field of social inclusion and mental health, although it is often not explicitly labelled as such. Part of the aim of social inclusion research is to pool current knowledge and best practice, in order to make people aware of work being done, to avoid duplication or conflict, and to promote 'best value' and effectiveness of existing approaches.

It is becoming clear that the promotion of social inclusion in mental health will probably best be achieved by a mixture of legal reform, media and educational work, and local service provision (Miller 1999; Sayce and Morris 1998; Sayce and Measey 1999). This section broadly outlines existing research and examples of good practice in all three of these categories, including some examples from outside the UK. It also refers in passing to inclusion work undertaken by and on behalf of other groups – such as minority ethnic communities, lesbians and gays, and people with learning disabilities or special needs. As in Chapter 1, we range across the key fields of employment, education and training, arts and the media, daily living, and mental health services.

Employment

The importance of promoting access to employment in order to promote social inclusion is emphasised by many in the mental health field, and is in accord with the current Government's understanding of social exclusion as primarily triggered by long-term unemployment.

Recent legal measures affecting employment practice for people with mental ill-health, as well as examples of gay and minority ethnic anti-discrimination work in the employment field, all shed light on 'what works' in reducing social exclusion.

Legal reform

We have referred already to some of the shortcomings of the Disability Discrimination Act (DDA) 1995 (see section 1.2 p. 16), but it is nonetheless a benchmark piece of legislation in signalling, to employers in particular, that certain discriminatory behaviours towards people with mental health problems are unacceptable. The way in which the employer's duty to make 'reasonable adjustments' is framed in Part II of the Act, and in guidance issued under it, illustrates how it is possible to insist on obligations in a flexible way, and to ensure some degree of protection not previously available to people experiencing mental ill-health. In October 1998 the Employment Appeal Tribunal delivered a landmark decision that will help employees with clinically diagnosed mental health problems to claim protection under the DDA (Sulek 1999). Mind supported this case, and has prioritised taking other test cases under the new law. Mental health practitioners are being encouraged to familiarise themselves with the DDA and the contribution it can make to support and rehabilitation. (Glozier 1999)

In the United States according to Sayce (1997), 'the Americans with Disabilities Act (ADA) 1990, which explicitly applies to people with psychiatric as well as physical impairments, has already become a lever for change'. The ADA is more comprehensive than the DDA, and US employers now know that they cannot refuse someone a job just because of a disability, and must make 'reasonable accommodation' in the workplace to ensure access. Employers also have access to literature and helplines to inform them how to do this. For example 'the mental health equivalent of the wheelchair ramp might be more regular feedback, or a buddy support system at work, or short breaks at times of distress (similar to a cigarette break), with the time made up later' (Sayce 1997). The ADA has proved to be a 'way in' to educating employers about how reasonable adjustments can be made for psychiatric disability. Service users, advocates and trainers have effectively influenced a number of employers through advice, helplines and training courses (Mancuso 1993). In Germany, quotas for the employment of disabled employees have been established, accompanied by financial penalties if employers do not comply – the monies raised are ploughed back into enhancing job opportunities for disabled people.

In the UK, welfare to work programmes have been introduced, starting with the New Deal in 1998. Experience from the USA suggests that keys to the success of welfare to work initiatives are the absence of compulsion – coercion and threats to benefits and welfare as a result of non-compliance do not promote mental health – and the reduction of benefit disincentives. For people with mental health problems, who may experience their ill-health episodically, the current UK benefits system can mean a net loss of income if they try work, become ill, and then have to reapply for benefits. (Extending the benefit linking rules to one year has ameliorated some of these problems, but not totally removed service users' insecurity.) There are also conflicting messages being given by New Deal and benefit entitlement checks – the All Work Test in particular has been criticised as unnecessarily threatening (Grove 1998).

A useful pointer to the effect of inclusive equal opportunities policies, and potential allies in achieving them, has been the experience of lesbian and gay men in the labour market. Research by the lobbying group Stonewall (Palmer 1993) showed that where an employer had an equal opportunities policy that included sexuality, 42 per cent of employees were 'out' at work about their sexuality. Amongst employers who did not have a policy, only 21 per cent felt able to be open. Good equal opportunities policies were much more common in the public and voluntary sector than the private sector, and the respondents felt that trades unions had played a key role in the spread of equal opportunities policies.

Other useful parallels with reference to inclusive employment are found in the work of the Commission for Racial Equality (CRE), established with the introduction of the Race Relations Act (RRA) 1976. A Code of Practice to the RRA that came into effect in 1984 provides a framework for employers to implement equal opportunities policies. The CRE set out persuading reluctant employers of the importance of meeting the Code by demonstrating the Code's recommendations were good personnel practice, and as such leading employers would want to implement them. They held a series of conferences, visited leading employers, and worked with umbrella organisations such as the Confederation for British Industry and the Institute for Personnel Management (CRE 1998).

In 1994 the Department of Employment (DoE) asked employers who had made positive action towards employing more staff from minority ethnic groups what had influenced them. Eighty-eight per cent of those surveyed said the decision to take positive action was taken at board level or by the chief executive, and that the CRE was the most common outside influence. Employers were also influenced by the DoE's Race Relations Employment Advisory Service (Welsh *et al.* 1994). Such research backs up support for the vital role the proposed Disability Rights Commission can play in employment, as well as other areas covered by DDA legislation. In addition it restates the case for giving the DDA more, and bigger, 'teeth'.

Supported employment

Controlled trials of US supported employment programmes for people with severe mental health problems show that unemployment can be halved by programmes that provide support 'on the job' (Bond *et al.* 1997), and there is emerging evidence that supported employment is cost-effective in the UK (Grove *et al.* 1997).

Some NHS trusts are addressing employment issues, and successful outcomes are beginning to emerge. Lewisham and Guy's NHS Trust have developed a 'partnership spectrum' for employment support, which integrates the health trust with a range of other agencies, from the Employment Service to Training and Enterprise Councils (TECs), to enable them to serve mental health clients with varying needs for support. By mid-1998, 236 vocational places had been provided to long-term service users in a variety of settings (*Lewisham and Guy's NHS Trust 1998/9 Business Plan*, quoted in Sayce and Morris 1998).

The South West London and St George's Mental Health NHS Trust (formerly Pathfinder) User Employment Project, modelled on successful projects in the United States, recruits people with mental health problems to ordinary jobs within the trust, and offers the necessary support. Personal experience of mental health problems is viewed as an asset for mental health work. Specific strategies put in place included:

- offering posts half-time in recognition of the transition for most applicants from long-term unemployment;
- acceptance of references from a GP or other health professional;
- extensive support in the recruitment process, e.g. open afternoons to help with application forms, guidelines and training for job interviews;
- support on the job, including a mentor colleague, and clear distinctions between job support, ordinary supervision at work and psychiatric treatment;
- flexible support, including morning telephone calls to help people get up, or help with childcare (Perkins *et al.* 1997).

Education and training

The recognition that processes of exclusion start at an early age saw the Government's Social Exclusion Unit focus on truancy and school exclusions as one of its early priorities (SEU 1998; SEU 1999). Work on exclusion in the school setting has also been undertaken for many years by the 'inclusion movement', which has lobbied for children with disabilities or 'special needs' to be included within mainstream education. There are many useful lessons to be learned and applied to the mental health field.

Inclusive education

Those who advocate specialist education for children with learning difficulties, physical or sensory impairments or behavioural difficulties argue that is it for the benefit of the children, as their 'special needs' will best be met through specialist education. However, opponents argue that separation is for the benefit of the mainstream, because of fears that 'special needs' children will affect the quality of education available for the majority.

Separate schools cost a lot and do not achieve good educational results. Perhaps most importantly, there is evidence that being schooled separately is bad for self-image, long-term social functioning and social access, and allows mainstream children, teachers and parents to remain in ignorance about disability.

> Continued segregation of disabled and non-disabled pupils can only help to foster stereotypes. Fear of disability by non-disabled people has its roots, at least in part, in the denied relationships of earlier years. Adults who have been educated within the special schools system often identify early segregation as the key factor in creating conditions that lead to prejudice and barriers in later life' (Centre for Studies in Inclusive Education 1996).

There is much research to show that children do better academically and socially in ordinary schools, and that integration adds to mainstream schools' strength and enhances the provision for all children. The role of inclusive education in combating discrimination and creating welcoming communities and an inclusive society has been recognised by UNESCO: 'Mainstream schools with an inclusive orientation are the most effective means of combating discriminatory attitudes and building an inclusive society' (UNESCO 1994).

Researching the process of educational inclusion in one London borough, Clough and Lindsay (1991) found that many teachers and local authority education staff initially thought school inclusion would be difficult, as did many parents. However, as the process went on they changed their minds, and eventually were in agreement that if sufficient support is provided all special educational needs children should be in the mainstream. Well organised courses for the teachers, aimed at explaining and supporting work towards integration, were vital in this process.

There have been concerns that inclusion of children with behavioural difficulties in mainstream schools might result in greater exclusion of individuals from schools for disciplinary reasons. This concern is set against a backdrop of a national trend of increasing exclusions. Merton Education Authority experienced a sharp increase in exclusions in the early 1990s. Rather than backing away from inclusive education, they decided to implement a more inclusive approach to behaviour support. This included establishing a lead support service to concentrate on preventative project work on behaviour issues, rather than individual support. They closed the local education authority's off-site unit for excluded pupils and set up mainstream provision; the special school for primary pupils with behavioural problems was replaced with high levels of multi-disciplinary support within mainstream classes. Behaviour support work was implemented at three levels – school, class and individual pupil – and goals, time limits and responsibilities for behaviour support projects were established through a 'partnership planning' process (Barrow 1998). By 1996/7 there was a significant decline in school exclusions.

A recent report by the National Association for the Care and Resettlement of Offenders (NACRO 1999) highlights several case-studies of schools undertaking innovative work to support children experiencing stress. The One for One project at a primary school in Bournemouth trains local unemployed people to provide extra learning support for 5–11 year olds showing signs of behavioural or learning difficulties; support is provided within the normal classroom routine, so as not to exclude the child. The Place to Be, a charity since 1994, is based in 11 schools in Camden, Southwark and Lewisham; school project workers based in each school manage the work of volunteers across a range of therapies, including art therapy, psychotherapy and drama therapy. The Place to Be offers provision that is accessible and does not have the stigma of mental health centres, and helps both pupils and schools as a whole. One school has seen a 34 per cent reduction in the number of pupils on the special educational needs register.

There are many lessons here for the specific mental health context, perhaps most notably:

- segregation and labelling, even if done with good intentions, can cause problems in themselves, including loss of self-esteem and stigmatisation;
- inclusion can help develop an awareness of diversity;
- the focus must be on abilities rather than disabilities;
- it is necessary to gain the confidence of all the 'stakeholders' – whether parents, teachers and pupils, or carers, mental health professionals and service users – by proper preparation, training and appropriate back-up.

Mental health promotion in schools

Specific mental health work in schools and other educational settings is still relatively in its infancy. Some schools are undertaking mental health awareness as part of the GCSE curriculum. The Health Education Authority/Health Development Agency has done some pioneering work in this regard, as have Mind and the Manic Depression Fellowship. For example Mind and the then HEA ran a 'Why use labels when they don't fit?' postcard campaign (Mind/HEA 1998). Nearly one million cards were distributed to schools and further education bodies across the country. Shoutlines such as 'psycho' and 'nutter' overlay photographic portraits of a variety of young men and women, while the back of the postcard depicted the 'real' stories behind such damaging labels. Mind followed this up with *The Bird and the Word,* a schools pack for 14–19 year olds opening up a variety of topics about mental health, stigma and discrimination, which has been enthusiastically adopted by over a thousand schools in under two years (Mind 1998).

The Manic Depression Fellowship (MDF) Wales has been operating a Lottery-funded education project in Welsh schools and colleges since 1997. Its main aim is to challenge the stigma and misinformation associated with mental health problems. Lectures and seminars are delivered by MDF members who use specially produced video and printed resources to open up discussion.

The Health Education Authority/Health Development Agency produces a range of materials for schools as part of World Mental Health Day. These include activity sheets for primary school children, and a survival diary for teenagers, with ideas about positive steps for improving mental health, such as talking or writing about your feelings, keeping in touch with friends and being prepared to ask for help (Friedli and Scherzer 1996; Rickford 1997)

In higher education, there are some innovative schemes aimed at students who are experiencing or have experienced mental health problems. For example Sandwell College in the west Midlands, as part of its mental health provision, has designed a course which offers people with mental health difficulties the opportunity to use the educational framework to explore their experiences. The course has been running for two academic years and has moved from being a predominantly day-centre-based class to a campus-based one. The 'academic feel' gained has been very much welcomed by the students, who look at the question, 'What is mental illness?' from a variety of different standpoints, as well as developing study skills, interpersonal and group skills (Austin 1999).

Arts and media
Some of the most original inclusion work in mental health in recent years has been in the arts. Projects have used the arts as a means to foster involvement and participation, and as 'agitprop', often at the same time. As evidence of the damaging effect of media coverage of mental health problems has grown (see Chapter 1), the arts have provided important avenues for conveying a different message.

Some groups have also intervened directly in the media industry, by promoting the voices of service users in the press, by encouraging service users and others to complain about misinformed reporting, and by a variety of other rebuttal techniques.

Drama
Drama is a powerful route both to empowerment and to getting across a message. The Act-up Drama Group in Dudley was formed in 1993 by a drama therapist at the suggestion of a client in hospital. The group explores mental health issues from the user perspective, and performs both to other users, for example in day centres, and also to professionals such as the police and teachers. The group has a committed core of performers who have stayed together, and it now has part-time funding as well as health authority interest and support. It also looks to involve others with acting skills – for example drama students or volunteer actors to support and sustain the group (Callanan *et al.* 1997).

Theatr Fforwm Cymru, based in Goodwick in Pembrokeshire, uses 'theatre of the oppressed' techniques (see p. 94) to involve the audience directly in health and social issues, including drug misuse, sexuality, bullying or stress. The actors devise a play showing the 'worst' aspects of a theme. On a second showing the audience or 'spectators' are asked to identify specifically with the protagonist, and to redirect the action to change the outcomes. The work is investigative and non-prescriptive, aimed at encouraging personal responsibility and empowerment. Theatr Fforwm Cymru involves mental health service users in the design and delivery of training sessions for service providers.

Arts and mental health work has a long history, but has tended to be fragmented and widely varying in different regions, often dependent on the enthusiasm and skills of individuals. Renewed interest in both the therapeutic *and* participative powers of the arts has encouraged a new vigour in the field. There have been attempts, such as that by the Arts and Mental Health Forum, to create a national network of arts and mental health projects, to encourage good practice, dissemination and coordinated resource planning. The King's Fund has developed an evaluation framework for art-based health work, which was pioneered in partnership with the Looking Well Centre, an arts-based community project in North Yorkshire (Angus and Murray 1996; Winn-Owen 1998; Friedli 1999).

Media

Media work in mental health has taken a two-pronged approach – challenging inaccurate or bigoted media portrayals of those with mental health problems, and promoting the voices of users and their allies directly in the press. Pioneering in the first of these approaches was the US National Stigma Clearing House, which used information technology to connect and mobilise a network of individuals to complain about – or sometimes to praise – TV and film producers and journalists.

In the UK a consortium of mental heath groups including Mind, the Mental Health Foundation, the National Schizophrenia Fellowship, the Manic Depression Fellowship, the Mental After Care Association and Mental Health Media formed Mediawatch in 1996. Mediawatch monitors mental health reporting and mobilises its supporters – users, carers and other concerned individuals and groups – to complain by post and phone about mental health stories in the media. This includes soaps and dramas as well as news and current affairs.

London-based Mental Health Media are currently producing a CD-Rom and website resource for journalists to give them access to correct information and the user perspective on mental health issues. MHM also produce mental health video and training resources for teachers and other professionals, and are constructing an oral history archive recording the experiences of mental health service users in the 20th century. The collection will be held in the National Oral History Archive at the British Museum.

Manchester's Schizophrenia Media Agency was set up by people who have been diagnosed with schizophrenia to improve the media representation of others with the diagnosis. The prime aim of SMA is to provide the media with articulate and trained interviewees. Successful contacts have been made with Radios 4 and 5, Channel 4 and *Hello, Marie Claire* and the *Big Issue,* amongst many others (SMA 1999).

Media work needs to be highly strategic in message and medium. In New Zealand a national campaign was launched on the back of market research testing the public's receptiveness to different messages and media. Subsequent linked initiatives involved a TV documentary about an MP who is open about her mental health problems, a book of 'stories of recovery', and media monitoring (Sayce 1997).

Mental health work in the media has become increasingly sophisticated in recent years, with many people working to use the media to promote positive mental health stories and also to give people information they need about help. However, more, and constant, work is needed to uncouple the potent association in the minds of the general public between violence and mental ill-health.

Daily living: access to goods, services and social networks

As we saw in Chapter 1, there are many ways in which experiencing mental health problems can exclude people from everyday experiences others take for granted. Some of these need to be addressed directly by mental health services, but others involve initiatives outside the mental health field, including legal reform and local community-based initiatives.

Legal reforms

Once again the Disability Discrimination Act can have impact in this area. The DDA makes it unlawful to treat disabled people less favourably in the provision of 'goods, facilities and services'; these are defined in a open-ended fashion, and include access to and use of the health service, the judicial system (except jury service – see p. 59), libraries, restaurants, conference centres, petrol stations and so on. The selling or letting of premises is also covered by the Act, as are services that grant loans and mortgages (Clements 1998). In the United States, the Americans with Disabilities Act 1990 has been used to establish that blanket refusal of driving licences to people with a history of mental health problems is unlawful (Mancuso 1993).

Community-based initiatives

We deal with countering nimbyism in the next section (p. 78), but it is worth noting here that one of the most effective rebuttals to nimbyism has been shown to be the involvement of service users in the everyday activities of local communities. Commentators have pointed out that if user groups, backed by mental health services, ensure that users have a presence in everything from local gyms to churches, women's groups to evening classes, then prejudice begins to break down at the grass roots (Repper *et al.* 1997; Sayce 1997).

We have discussed in Chapters 1 and 2 the importance of economics in shaping the daily lives of people with mental health problems, and there are several well-known examples of LETS (local exchange trading schemes) that have had a dramatic impact on people's lives (Croall 1997). One such example is Beckford Community LETS in Warminster. Based in a community centre, the scheme has around fifty members, one third of them are current users of mental health services, one third have used them in the past, and one third have had no contact with mental health services. This scheme has a number of particularly successful features, notably its inclusive mix of members, an ethos of mutual collaboration, an assertive approach to community co-operation, positive relationships with GPs, a complementary therapies focus, and an emphasis on general health promotion (for example an organic freezer food project, exercise groups) (Callanan *et al.* 1997).

In Aston near Birmingham, an innovative craft project for Asian women has proved to have great potential as a tool for inclusion. A textile artist at Birmingham Central Museum and Art Gallery with a longstanding interest in Indian art set up an embroidery group for Indian women. Embroidery is an important part of Indian women's cultural heritage, and the aim was to bring women into the Museum – 'a place of beauty' – and create a social context which allowed them to engage with one another and regain a part of their cultural heritage. The Asian Women's Textile Group was perceived as a form of preventative health care, addressing isolation and loneliness amongst local Indian women, but many of the women were already on medication, and some reduced their medication dramatically after coming to the group. The embroidery itself, the social contact, the venue and the end-product (the tapestries have been displayed in galleries in Birmingham and Aston) were all seen as greatly boosting self-esteem (Callanan *et al.* 1997).

There are many local initiatives that take inclusion for granted in their guiding principles. For example Bromley-by-Bow community centre in the

East End of London, established 15 years ago, has evolved dynamically with inclusiveness as one of its cornerstones, and people with mental health problems are fully integrated into the centre's work. The centre includes a nursery, café, dance school and health project as well as groups for minority ethnic women and people with disabilities. The aim is always to 'push power down', so the nursery is run by parents and the café is run by local people as a business (Callanan *et al.* 1997). If social inclusion work is to succeed, then the contribution and importance of community initiatives such as these, as complementary partners to specific mental health services, cannot be overstated.

Mental health services and health education

While it is vital that mental health service providers acknowledge and support inclusion work outside their traditional boundaries, it is equally clear that the lead responsibility to promote social inclusion for people with mental health problems must lie with mental health services themselves. As we have seen, some commentators argue that mental health services have unwittingly contributed to the exclusion of those they seek to help (see pp. 29–30), and it is these processes that must be reversed, both by internal culture change and reorientation of external services.

Inclusive community-based services

Psychiatric services that are moving towards inclusion can set in motion a kind of sea change in psychiatric culture. Inclusion requires a re-evaluation of the biomedical model of mental health and illness, which defines mental illness as that which places an individual outside the societal norm. Link *et al.* (1997) have noted that even when diagnosis leads to effective treatment of symptoms within conventional psychiatry, the stigma associated with the diagnosis continues. They also found that the continuing stigma is associated with the recurrence of mental health problems. As Sayce points out (1998), this has 'far-reaching implications for discussions of clinical effectiveness: a narrow emphasis on symptom reduction will not address discrimination, and discrimination itself forms part of the experience of mental health problems. Clinicians need to understand mental health problems *in relation* to the disabling effects of discrimination.' Perkins and Repper (1996) have produced an analysis of how clinical practice can be developed on the basis of working alongside people with serious mental health problems, to support them in gaining access to their communities of choice.

One example of this approach is the Bradford Home Treatment team, set up three years ago. The team consists of support workers, nurses, a social worker and a clinical medical officer, plus input from two psychiatrists and a service-user development worker (Bracken and Thomas 1999). The team works on a 24-hour basis and patients are visited at home every day; the service has been very successful in reducing the demand for inpatient care, and feedback from users is very positive.

Good community-based services have been shown time and again to reduce the need for acute inpatient care, an outcome to everyone's advantage. Julian Housing Support, a Norwich-based community housing organisation for people with mental health problems, was able to disband its crisis helpline because of lack of demand. Active outreach teams emphasise prevention rather than cure, and practical help with finances, housing and social integration are seen as the fundamentals. With more than 350 clients, Julian Housing has seen only two short unplanned admissions in the last two years (Sheldon 1999).

Using similar principles in the general health context, Stockport Healthcare NHS Trust created six community health worker posts to work directly with local communities in deprived areas. The aim was to enable the local people to identify their health and social needs, and design localised solutions. Mental health is integral to everything the health workers (mostly former health visitors) do. Recent projects include the 'Feel Good Factory', jointly run with Stockport Mind, which had a creche, relaxation classes and dance classes amongst its facilities. The community health workers feed into the local health authority's strategy via 16 neighbourhood health strategy projects, and the workers have active commitment and support from senior managers in both the trust and the health authority (Callanan *et al.* 1997).

Acute care

Even with increasing attention paid to prevention and community-based support, inpatient care is, and needs to remain, an integral part of the mental health services. Criticisms of mainstream acute psychiatric care are many and varied (Moore and McCulloch 1998; Hart 1999), and many users have called for wider availability of crisis services (Mental Health Foundation 1999) as an alternative to hospital. Drayton Park is one such service, run by women for women in Islington, north London. It is an alternative to hospital, aiming to provide the 'place of safety' many users want in times of acute crisis. Users are offered a bed for up to a month, the surroundings are as homely and 'non-institutional' as possible, and the emphasis is on high-quality care with staff having time to talk to and listen to the residents (Wells 1999).

User involvement

All effective services have a high degree of user involvement. Facilitating user involvement is a vital part of progressive psychiatric services, enshrined in Government health policy, but its implementation is erratic and patchy. There is increasing demand for user input, but not enough attention paid to supporting it. Some innovative schemes are training users to be trainers, so that their input is formalised and properly recognised.

The Capital Project, set up by West Sussex Social Services in 1998, trained 13 users in its first year in skills needed to provide professional training days for mental health workers. In their first year these user-trainers ran over 30 sessions for over 400 mental health workers. Similarly Users as Trainers set up a ten-day course in Glamorgan in early 1998 to offer users the chance to learn training and presentation skills, network with other user-trainers and increase their knowledge of how mental health professionals are trained.

Over and above this, as we have already noted, some mental health trusts are leading the way in recognising the contribution to be made by service users employed within mental health services (see section 3.1 p. 68).

Challenging nimbyism

Performance indicators are becoming important engines driving decisions in mental health policy and strategic planning, and attention is being paid in some areas as to how they relate to issues of social inclusion. For example, in the South and North Thames area the NHS Executive has piloted performance indicators based on Mind's good practice guidelines for challenging nimbyism (Sayce and Willmot 1997). The Mind guidelines suggest that services can and should encourage and sustain constructive relations between users and local communities. This can be done by supporting users in advocating for themselves, forming active relationships with local colleges, churches and other groups, pro-active work with local media, and supporting user-led education in schools and other venues (Sayce 1998). Performance indicators that put inclusion at the heart of mental health services' aims and outcomes can begin to shift the terrain towards truly community-oriented mental health services. Providers should also be helped in these endeavours by provisions of the Disability Discrimination Act that make it unlawful for any person to aid, abet or incite others to discriminate against a disabled person. As the letting and selling of premises is covered by the DDA, nimby protesters may be acting unlawfully if they put pressure on a local authority not to grant planning permission, or a building society or landowner not to sell or let a building (Clements 1998).

Mental health promotion and education

A lot of inclusion work takes the form of public education, whether at local or national level, but this is an area in urgent need of more research, resources and planning. The then Health Education Authority previously commented that there was a 'critical absence of evidence on programmes concerned with the social and economic determinants of mental health. There is a strong need to support more research in areas like housing, inequality and discrimination' (Tilford *et al.* 1997). The Health Development Agency, successor to the Health Education Authority, now has mental health firmly within its brief (DoH 1999) (Friedli 1999; Friedli and Scherzer 1996).

Mind's 1996–9 'Respect' campaign highlighted many of the issues of discrimination and exclusion users experience, with its two reports on discrimination receiving over 300 sympathetic mentions in national and local media (Read and Baker 1996; Repper *et al.* 1997).

While statutory and professional bodies have been slower to address discrimination issues, there is progress. The Royal College of Psychiatrists' ongoing campaign 'Changing Minds: Every Family in the Land' sets out explicitly to combat stigma by 'increasing public understanding of mental disorders and challenging society's preconceptions' (RCP 1998).

On a more local level, agencies such as the Powys Agency for Mental Health have coordinated multi-agency mental health promotion and public awareness campaigns. PAMH worked with local groups such as the Farmers' Union, women's groups, the local press and local schools in educational activities aimed at reducing the stigma attached to mental ill-health and promote positive mental wellbeing.

Public education can make a big difference. The Australian Department of Health ran a poster campaign of a footballer scoring above the caption 'The defense didn't stop him; neither did mental illness', and research showed some alteration in people's attitudes as a result. Campaigns in New Zealand and the United States have also shown that carefully targeted and planned promotion and education can alter public perceptions of mental health problems (Sayce 1998).

3.2 Evidence presented to the Inquiry

Having heard powerful firsthand evidence of the social exclusion experienced by people with mental health problems (section 1.2 p. 11), the Inquiry Panel went on to hear witnesses testifying on work promoting inclusion. The Panel heard a wide range of evidence about initiatives, both in mental health services and the wider community, that give cause for optimism. A lot is happening, positive effects are manifest and measurable, and the scope for dissemination is vast.

Employment

Exclusion from employment is seen by many as the key nut to crack, and a number of successful initiatives, some already mentioned in section 3.1, were brought to the Panel's attention. The obstacles to gaining work for mental health service users are manifold, but this does not mean that the solutions are necessarily hugely complex or impractical. What is necessary, however, is a culture-change – on the part of mental health services *and* employers.

There was much encouraging evidence from large employers who were witnesses at the Inquiry. It was clear that they took the mental wellbeing of their existing employees very seriously:

> Our occupational health people are now very keen to develop rehabilitation programmes. If somebody working with us develops a health problem then our impulse now is to try and retain that employee. This may involve adjustments to working practices, working hours, the tasks involved with that person's specific job. It may involve setting up support to help the person on a day-to-day basis – all the kinds of adjustments you would expect to make under the Disability Discrimination Act. Some areas also have local initiatives; for example some branches have employed a local massage expert to go on-site and give massage to employees. *Gale Issitt, HSBC*

> We offer a company counselling service, and promote rehabilitation and support for staff during and after illness, including mental health problems. We understand and subscribe to the suggestions for best practice with regard to mental health and employment, and are open to guidance on how best to further translate these into action. *Norwich Union (written evidence)*

The problem we face with mental health is understanding the implications of a particular mental health problem and therefore what reasonable adjustments might mean. However, our fair employment handbook refers specifically to mental health issues, and many of our member companies have trained employees as peer counsellors or 'listeners', who can provide fellow employees with confidential support on any issue, work related or not. We would hope that people with mental health problems would seek and find support through this system. It may involve setting up support to help the person on a day-to-day basis – all the kinds of adjustments you would expect to make under the DDA. Some areas have local initiatives; for example some branches have employed a local massage expert to give on-site massage to employees. *Northern Foods (written evidence)*

We have an 'Open Line' service, which is an independent, confidential counselling service open to all employees. *Chrissie Lawson, Tesco*

Many employers spoke of trying to prevent stress building up in employees, recognising that this can lead to mental health problems. When problems do arise, some companies are becoming more willing to look at their own role in creating them. One witness from a large employer spoke of a case where a senior employee with a previously excellent record was found to be stealing from the company. The company initially decided to get the police involved, despite being told that the employee was under great mental stress at work. The employee then made a suicide attempt, which caused the company completely to re-evaluate their response, including whether their handling of the situation had contributed to the person's attempt to take their own life. They subsequently dropped all police and disciplinary actions, and set about working with the employee, the employee's doctor and the occupational health department with a view to eventually re-employing the individual at the same level of seniority.

This culture change is not necessarily about ethical responsibilities, though for some companies these are very important. It is also a recognition that it may be more cost-effective to support staff through problems and to try and retain them, rather than incurring the cost of replacing them. The Panel heard, for example, from one large high-street company that made adjustments to accommodate employees diagnosed with schizophrenia, including changing shifts to facilitate access to health care.

However, it was clear from previous evidence (see section 1.2 p. 11) that problems begin at the recruitment stage. Many witnesses called for various changes and additions to the Disability Discrimination Act, and some witnesses felt that using the DDA to improve chances of recruitment was one of the biggest single changes that could be made in the field of employment:

> I want to see a law that restricts the employer's ability to discriminate prior to appointment. I think that's extremely important. There needs to be a restriction on employers asking questions on application forms and at interview about people's medical histories. You need to give people a chance to prove themselves in interviews before you get around to any discussion about mental health problems. *Caroline Gooding, Employers' Forum on Disability*

> We need a good all round 'thou shalt not discriminate' law that has lots of teeth. *Leeds Mental Health Advocacy Group (written evidence)*

In addition, employers tended to look at mental health from two angles – the employee angle, as outlined, and the customer service angle. The business case for not discriminating against any customers – including those with mental health problems – is slowly percolating through (see also section 3.2 p. 95). And when it comes to 'customer service' issues within the National Health Service, this has particular implications for recruitment:

> In employment in the mental health arena it obviously makes sense for mental health service providers to be employing their customers; changing the system. *Caroline Gooding, Employers' Forum on Disability*

> There are two key areas of benefit in employing people with mental health problems within mental health services. First, work opportunities for people with serious mental health problems are increased, which has been shown to improve health. Second, the quality of care offered by the service is improved: clients benefit from the advice and expertise of user employees who have 'been there' themselves. *Rachel Perkins, South West London and St George's Mental Health NHS Trust*

Confidentiality and disclosure issues are very sensitive with regard to mental health, a point of great concern for mental health service users and one on which employers felt they needed guidance. Several witnesses suggested these issues could actually resolve themselves if a relatively simple perception shift – one that parallels the perception shift needed within psychiatry – is instilled. This is the shift away from *diagnosis*, towards addressing *practical needs:*

> Really, at work, occupational health should disappear from view, because the employee is talking to their manager in a work setting, about practical needs in relation to their working conditions. Here is an example from an educational setting, but it applies equally to work. A young woman wanted to go to college. The bridge-builder [worker facilitating inclusion, see p. 102] asked if the young woman thought the tutor should know something about her background. 'Yeah, tell her I'm schizophrenic,' said the woman. The bridge-builder asked why, and eventually it became clear that because her medication was tranquillising the woman thought she might be late for class sometimes. So all the tutor needed to know was that their student might be late to class sometimes because she's taking medication. The bridge-builder supported the young woman to write a letter about this to the tutor, so that she still owned the information, and chose to disclose it. *Peter Bates, National Development Team*

Witnesses made important points (parallel with the CRE's argument about good policies on minority ethnic employees, see p. 67) about employers being persuaded that creating good conditions for people with mental health problems means creating good working conditions *per se.* Addressing mental health properly means *all* your staff will feel better, so it's in your interests as a competitive employer to do it:

> It's important to remember that very often 'reasonable adjustments' as required in the DDA here and the ADA in the United States, are positive all round. Although I am not aware of any specific research on the subject, anecdotally you hear of the benefits that openness about mental health issues can bring to a workplace. So that if somebody feels confident about talking about their diagnosis it improves the communication flow generally. If

you create a climate that is conducive to employees with mental
health problems, chances are it will be a good climate anyway.
Caroline Gooding, Employers' Forum on Disability

However, despite the strength of the case for encouraging employers not
to discriminate on the grounds of mental ill-health, the current lack of focus
on employment *within mental health services* was seen as a real impediment
to change:

Many health providers would challenge the idea that they have any
role in employment issues. But without our input people will be
denied opportunities that can significantly impact on their mental
health. *Tony Coggins, Lewisham and Guy's Mental Health Trust*

(See section 3.2 p. 99 for further evidence regarding good practice in
employment within mental health services.)

The National Health Service generally should be leading the way as a
responsible and inclusive employer, above and beyond the specific issues
about employment within the mental health services:

The NHS is the biggest employer in the country, and it's simply up to
us to ensure that we are good employers and inclusive employers.
Voirrey Manson, NHS Equality Unit

If in the health services we are going to look to outside employers
to employ people who've experienced mental health difficulties,
we jolly well ought to put our own house in order first. It is not
reasonable for me as a mental health service provider to go to
Sainsbury's and say please employ someone if I'm not actually
employing someone myself. *Rachel Perkins, South West London and
St George's Mental Health NHS Trust*

The raft of new Government health initiatives is an ideal vehicle for
encouraging fair employment practices within health and social services.
For example, as one Community Health Council commented, all
organisations that sign up to a Health Action Zone (see Glossary) should
have fair employment policies that specifically include references to
mental health.

The need for a single authoritative voice on the question of mental health and employment was highlighted often by witnesses from the commercial, voluntary and private sectors. One witness summed this up:

> We really need a single body, which employers can work in partnership with, that permeates through the mental health system and through the employers' systems, private, statutory and voluntary. At the moment, people don't know who to go to for information and advice. *Caroline Gooding, Employers' Forum on Disability*

Crucially, welfare and benefit reforms need to go hand in hand with employment reform:

> If you asked me what is the one big change that needs to be made to encourage people with mental health problems into work, it is to change the benefits system – to get rid of the many disincentives that mean it is financially impossible for people to try working. *Tony Coggins, Lewisham and Guy's Mental Health Trust*

> It's about joined-up government, isn't it? Making sure that the Department for Social Security isn't working against what the Department of Employment might be trying to achieve. We need to look carefully at welfare to work and to dovetail all these measures with sensible changes to the benefits system. Everyone stands to gain from this. *Rachel Perkins, South West London and St George's Mental Health NHS Trust*

One aspect of benefit reform is to provide clear, non-punitive rationales for benefit qualifications, which do not remove benefits too early or keep people out of work unnecessarily. The corollary to this process within the employment sphere is being clear and realistic about people's capabilities of working, so that they are not set up to fail:

> Agencies promoting work for people with mental health problems need to be clear about when someone is or is not job-ready. There will be times when people aren't ready for mainstream work, but where it would be helpful for them to have a job which is more therapeutic and may then lead to a fully active job. *Caroline Gooding, Employers' Forum on Disability*

Finally, working with rather than against employers was also fundamental:

> There's quite a lot of antagonism towards employers – and this isn't just within mental health but within the disability field generally. Employers are seen as the enemy. Sometimes this is with very good reason, because people have had awful experiences. But you can't engage employers in trying to change employment practice unless you understand their agenda as well. *Caroline Gooding, Employers' Forum on Disability*

Education and training

Evidence to the Inquiry in the education and training category concentrated mainly on the issues of fair access to mainstream services, and what form supported education and training should take.

Schools

Earlier witnesses testified to the damage done by the legally sanctioned segregation of disabled and non-disabled children in school (see section 1.2 p. 19 and section 3.1 p. 69). Schooling that rejects the exclusionary ethic can have an extremely positive impact on children's current and subsequent mental health, and as several witnesses told the Inquiry Panel, initiatives to promote it have much to teach mental health inclusion work for adults:

> Where we have been fortunate enough to find professionals willing and able to respond to the challenge of inclusion in schools, we have built something that has never happened before. We have built communities in which the most vulnerable and dependent members are put at the very centre, and are viewed as essential to the true education of a new generation.
>
> In some cases this has meant the literal rebuilding of school environments. It has also meant looking at every aspect of school policy, teaching methods, curriculum and staffing levels. It has brought more adults into the school as teachers' aides, welfare assistants, counsellors. It has acknowledged the enormous contributions children make to each other's learning, formalised in peer-tutoring and collaborative planning groups. It has put friendship high on the agenda, by talking about it and deliberately

setting up 'circles of support' around isolated children.

Truly inclusive schools do not exclude on the basis of emotional and behavioural disturbances, but try to help and understand what caused the child to 'act out'. In the very best examples 'flying services' have been developed, attached to school systems. These flying services can move between schools when called, offering support, not just to the child but to her or his family or carers, when it is needed. This is seen as 'preventative medicine', and is an example of using resources to bring together rather than separate. It is also economical in that two weeks' intervention of this kind often saves several years later on. It is the opposite of our 'not-until-a-crisis' support services. *Micheline Mason, Alliance for Inclusive Education*

In the network we have set up in Nottingham to promote inclusion for people with mental health problems there is also an educational psychologist working with children at risk of exclusion in special schools, and helping mainstream schools to become inclusive. *Peter Bates, National Development Team*

There's an example I really recommend people to look at in Plymouth. It was a failing junior school, for 7–11 year olds in a very run-down estate. Fifty per cent of the children had special educational needs. A new head teacher came in and decided two things had to happen: boundaries needed to be set so that children and adults both felt safe, and the children and adults needed to decide together what the boundaries were. The second thing was that the school needed to be made into a democracy: the pupils needed to be citizens who shared in the decision-making. So for example, the garden project becomes a joint pupil–teacher project, with children taking the initiative and helping to make the plans. In effect, the head decided it was time to stop bleating about lack of resources and treat the children themselves as the resource. Through circles of support, training the children in mediation skills, setting up guardian angel schemes, the school has been totally transformed – it has had no exclusions in the past two years. The children even interview and employ new teachers. As an example of giving control back to the young and promoting inclusion it is an outstanding model. *Micheline Mason, Alliance for Inclusive Education*

Further and higher education

In further and higher education there is not an officially and legally sanctioned segregation of students, but (see section 1.2 p. 17) there is still exclusion:

> To some extent within further and higher education we are working with a better situation than schools – we're not trying to fight against an existing legally segregated system. However, there is still exclusion and it is difficult to overcome this. The whole system is set up with the view 'we provide and you can fit in, but if you don't you can drop out'. *Sophie Corlett, Skill – National Bureau for Students with Disabilities*

Where disability access work has been going on, it has tended to focus on physical barriers:

> Recent emphasis within higher education on the needs and abilities of students with disabilities has focused on physical and environmental barriers. Further attention should be given to the needs of students with mental health problems as part of higher education's expressed aim to broaden access. Institutions need to be aware of the needs of students who enter education with a history of mental health problems, and to develop a strategic approach encompassing publicity materials, inquiries and applications, support staff and other students. An institution-wide approach is necessary. *Jill Manthorpe and Nicky Stanley, University of Hull (written evidence)*

In addition, several witnesses pointed out that college and university life can be the place where mental health problems start for many people – it is a stressful change, full of new pressures and different boundaries, and usually away from support networks of family and existing friends:

> For many people mental health problems begin at college or university, but the system is completely unable to cope with students when they do develop difficulties. *Sophie Corlett, Skill – National Bureau for Students with Disabilities*

> There is a great need for higher education institutions to develop and sustain support systems for students who develop mental

health problems during their student career. Such systems need to relate to local health services, and referral and communication routes need to be negotiated. In particular, students engaged in professional training need to be able to access help without fear that this will prejudice their career or professional progress. The professions themselves need to avoid being seen as unnecessarily judgmental and should be open about their procedures and views.
Jill Manthorpe and Nicky Stanley, University of Hull (written evidence)

Despite these widespread problems there is innovative work going on. One promising area is in helping people with pre-existing mental health problems to access specially designed and supported courses as a stepping-stone to mainstream education:

There are colleges that have looked at more imaginative ways of working. Often these have been starter courses for people who have had mental health problems and who want to get back into mainstream education. These are discrete short-term courses that don't necessarily aim to send people off with an NVQ, but aim to get people back into education. They are quite relaxed courses – where people can be with others who have had similar experiences – but in the mainstream sector so the students are going into the canteen, mixing with students on other courses and beginning to pick up relationships, make friends and operate within a wider social setting. This can then give them the confidence to progress on to a different, mainstream course.

The key thing about these courses is that they must be non-intimidating, run by people who understand about mental health problems, not demanding huge results at a certain time. They need to be courses that are really sensitive to students' needs, rather than expecting students to accommodate to the courses' needs. *Sophie Corlett, Skill – National Bureau for Students with Disabilities*

We've got something called a First Stage Access Course at Stoke Park School Community College in Coventry. People with mental health problems can go on this course and explore options, things they might like to study in a mainstream college environment. They get lunch provided, and it's a small discrete group. Once they are in the college environment they have a support worker, and they can go and sit in on different classes, take all the time they need throughout one academic year to decide what they might like to do within the college – no pressure.

We've also got a foundation course at Tarnhill College that used to be a course specifically for people with learning difficulties – the focus has changed. The recognition is there. This has happened partly because we've made links with other colleges who are trailblazers. For example Stepping Stones in Lancashire has six thousand students with mental health problems, some in specialist courses, some supported in the mainstream, and it's working. Then there's Mandela College in Leicestershire where part of the college is used two days a week for people with mental health problems to come and try lots of different courses. *Jan Turnbull, Coventry Social Services*

In Nottingham we formed an informal network of people working for inclusion – including bridge-builders, who ideally work full-time. A bridge-builder in further education has seen nearly one thousand mental health service users become students. *Peter Bates, National Development Team*

In 1993 Clarendon College in Nottingham set up a Mental Health Support Service. In the academic year 1996/7 there were 250 students being supported to attend classes within mental health centres, to attend classes for mental health service users in college, or attending mainstream provision. Part of the service has been the setting up of a mental health advisory group, made up of mental health support service staff, Clarendon College management, mental health workers and students. The purpose of this group is to raise concerns and inform good practice. Student participation has been vital in raising awareness of the support requirements of students with mental health difficulties and pushing forward the service. *Kathryn James, Clarendon College (written evidence)*

Themes already raised in relation to employment came up again: particularly emphasised was the need for another extension of the Disability Discrimination Act – to cover training and education (section 1.2 p. 17). Several witnesses drew attention to developing sensitive and coherent guidelines covering confidentiality in relation to medical histories (see section 3.1 p. 82).

Witnesses were agreed that while 'stepping-stones' and access courses were vital and must be supported and replicated across the country, the ultimate aim of inclusion work within further and higher education is the true inclusion of students with mental health problems into mainstream education:

> In inclusion work, people often mistake the mid-point for the end-point. For example in a college, if you set up a class for mental health service users only in the ordinary college, many projects think they've arrived. Now this is a good start, but it is only a stepping-stone. Mainstream registration alongside ordinary citizens is more like inclusion in my book. *Peter Bates, National Development Team*

As with all inclusion work, the lives and needs of students should be looked at in a holistic way:

> While much attention has focused on student suicide, other problems and issues connected to mental health have been far less visible. Further work is required to address the area of suicide and self-harm, but also to identify other outcomes and preventative strategies. Similarly, students' mental health problems are far more diverse than the stereotypical picture of an undergraduate facing examination stress. The particular needs of mature students, part-time students, international students and those from minority ethnic groups should be researched and addressed. *Jill Manthorpe and Nicky Stanley, University of Hull (written evidence)*

Underlying all attempts to promote access to training and education is the need to establish which agencies take responsibility for the work: close cooperation between social services, mental health services, both statutory and voluntary, and educational bodies is vital if this work is to be properly supported and replicated. Inclusion work in this field, just as in employment, is in dire need of 'joining-up'.

Arts and media

The Panel had already heard many witnesses implicate the media in fanning the flames of prejudice against mental health service users. In recent years there have been more, and increasingly sophisticated, initiatives to provide a corrective – both through mainstream media work and through various art forms (see section 3.1 p. 72).

Media work

Just as the media has done a good deal of damage, so it has potential to do a great deal of good:

> How do we change public attitudes? Well we can't give psychotherapy to 50 million people and get them to acknowledge their own violent and sexual impulses [see p. 50], but we can provide role models. And this is where the media has such enormous potential. *Julian Leff, Institute of Psychiatry*

> The answer to problems about mental health reporting is quite a simple one. We already have a set of conventions the news applies to, for example, counselling given to victims of trauma – rail crashes, bombings and so on. The scripts are sympathetic, the presenter's tone encourages understanding, the trauma is acknowledged and the counselling applauded. If news media was to reduce the generic elements in their reporting that mobilise moral panic about mental illness, and apply instead some of the norms associated with post-traumatic stress and counselling, then new and more accurate understandings about these mental health issues might have the space to emerge.
>
> In addition, the media can be positive in its images of mental health. The video diary *Mad, Sad or Bad* (BBC2 September 1994) was particularly powerful in portraying everyday life for someone with a schizophrenia diagnosis. *Takin' over the Asylum* (BBC2 August 1996) was an excellent example of how drama can bring sympathy, poignancy and humour to bear on the experiences of people with mental health problems. The *Eastenders* character Joe was also well researched and acted. Essentially, I believe the way forward for the media is to raise questions about mental health, to stimulate curiosity in audiences to find out the 'how' and the 'why' of mental health issues. *Mike Birch, Falmouth College of Arts*

The power of disclosure, of coming out, is very relevant in this media context. It was noted that the increasing number of people in the public eye willing and able to 'come out' as gay or lesbian was instrumental in the increasing public acceptance of homosexuality. Work in overthrowing the stigma attached to mental health problems is still very much in its infancy by comparison, but the effect of respected public figures discussing their mental health problems cannot be underestimated:

> If we had more famous people coming out as mental health services users it would go a long way to countering social exclusion. *Citizens Advice Bureau advocate (written evidence)*

> We really need the media to portray positive images of people with mental health problems, instead of continual scare-mongering. *community advocate (written evidence)*

Some international examples of effective media work were also presented to the Panel. In the Carter Center, in Atlanta, Georgia, there is a fellowship programme in mental health for mainstream journalists to ensure that they will be better informed when reporting on mental health issues. Lichtenstein Creative Media, an independent production company based in New York City, has created a public service announcement campaign containing anti-stigma and anti-discrimination messages related to mental health. A radio documentary series they produced, *Voices of Illness*, was hailed by the US National Institute of Mental Health as having 'truly set new standards of creativity and scientific accuracy in broadcast journalism about mental illness'. Stamp Out Stigma, another US initiative, is a speakers' bureau formed by people diagnosed with serious mental illness. They give brief, interactive presentations to diverse audiences, including a biographical sketch of how diagnosis has affected their lives, how they experience stigma, and how they have worked to change the perceptions of others (Mind 1998).

The arts

There are positives to be gained not only from the results of increased representation of people with mental health problems, but also from the process. Participation, a key theme in the ethical discussions between witnesses and the Panel (see section 2.2 p.59), is one of the driving determinants in mental health and arts work. According to a Joseph Rowntree Foundation conference on arts and community regeneration:

Arts-based programmes have been shown to contribute towards enhancing social cohesion and local image, building private–public sector partnerships, promoting an interest in the local environment, developing self-confidence, enhancing organisational capacity, supporting independence and exploring visions of the future. The use of the arts coincides with a shift in emphasis in regeneration strategies towards seeing local people as the principal asset through which renewal can be achieved (Wollheim 1996).

As witnesses to the Inquiry put it:

> We believe the arts can play a major role in developing excluded groups' confidence and ability to take an active role in their communities, and for the work they do through the arts to be a major tool in breaking down individuals' or communities' prejudice and preconceptions. *Theatre in Prisons and Probation Centres (written evidence)*

> There are many examples of arts in mental health work – for example the involvement of mental health service users by Nottingham Museum Service in education and outreach work which has been long and patient and very successful [see section 3.2 p. 97]. The people involved benefit in terms of personal confidence, by being included in activities that aren't presented as therapeutic, i.e. only targeted at them as service users. Then there is a significant impact on their social lives and confidence. *Francois Matarasso, Comedia*

Witnesses made reference to Augusto Boal, creator of the Latin American 'Theatre of the Oppressed', in which groups of citizens use drama and performance as a liberating and interactive process to highlight their experiences, often those of exclusion or discrimination:

> One of the British manifestations of the Theatre of the Oppressed is a company called Cardboard Citizens. This is a homeless people's theatre company that plays mainly in hostels and other venues for homeless people, and their plays address issues around homelessness – everything from resettlement to abuse. In this form of theatre they play a story through once, and then they start to

play it through again and they invite the audience to intervene – to say stop. Then a member of the audience comes into the play, takes the place of the protagonist and tries a different approach to see if they might get a different result. The work is about understanding the complexity of the oppressions people find themselves confronted with, and identifying opportunities and mechanisms for change, both for individuals and society. *Perry Walker, New Economics Foundation*

Theatre in Prisons and Probation aims to use drama to offer excluded groups an opportunity to open dialogue with their peers, their community and also those that might be prejudiced against them. In HMP Buckley Hall we run an employment module examining personal and social barriers to reintegration with soon-to-be-released prisoners. It culminates with a performance by prisoners to an audience of potential employers to open a debate as to how ex-prisoners can have full access to employment opportunities. *Theatre in Prisons and Probation Centres (written evidence)*

Within mental health services there is already considerable recognition of the important contribution that arts can make, but the issue of mid-points being mistaken for end-points, raised in relation to education (see section 3.2 p. 90), is also very pertinent here:

It's great when, for example, mental health projects get users'/survivors' poetry performed and published. This is so important in recognising people's strengths and abilities. But in terms of inclusion, it may not do anything in helping people who use psychiatric services build friendships with the local poetry society. *Peter Bates, National Development Team*

In sum, the arts, far beyond the narrow confines of 'art therapy', have a vital role to play in fostering inclusion. As one witness said:

The arts should not be seen as an end in themselves. I would prefer people to think of the arts as one of the tools humans have developed by which they change their circumstances or address the world. *Francois Matarasso, Comedia*

Daily living: access to goods, services and social networks

Within this very broad category the Panel previously heard selected examples of how exclusion can operate (see section 1.2 p. 20). Counter measures presented to the Panel again ranged very widely – from the Disability Discrimination Act, to customer charters, to befriending schemes.

Including consumers

The Panel heard how accessing everyday goods and services is made difficult for people with mental health problems (see section 1.2 p. 20), and in this section witnesses outline some of the ways in which these often insidious exclusions are being challenged.

The Disability Discrimination Act once more has a key role to play. Its widespread definition of the goods and services to which disabled people are legally required to have equal access has done much to make visible exclusionary practices of which many people were previously unaware (see section 3.1 p. 74).

Commercial pressures also play their part; there is a clear business case for making what you are selling available to all. One utility provider, for example, explained how they must demonstrate to the regulator that they are responsive to people's need: 'We have nine specific services for this circumstance, some of which might apply to people with mental health problems: a password scheme, so that people can be sure if one of our staff calls at their door that it is safe to let them in; a redirection scheme, which allows people who feel particularly vulnerable to have a named person accompany the staff member into the customer's house; and a third-party bill scheme for people not happy about handling their own bills.'

Innovative new ways of selling – particularly making use of new technology – can also help people with mental health problems. Witnesses commented that some people with mental health problems have found supermarket internet shopping, for example, to be a huge benefit. People who are housebound because of their distress can actually use some high-street supermarkets, via the internet, to do shopping at competitive prices and at times that they can manage. This is a tremendous improvement on, for example, local authority shopping services, which some witnesses found added to distress rather than alleviating it.

While a 'good business' approach can therefore be consonant with promoting inclusive access to the goods and services needed in everyday life, there were also witnesses who felt that the profit motive was one of the underlying factors creating social exclusion across society (see section 1.2, p.14 and 2.2, p. 50). Some witnesses therefore argued that truly successful moves towards inclusion must address this deeper issue:

One of the outcomes of profit-motivated economics is that we are being forced to re-buy as individuals what we once bought collectively. These include our nationalised industries, council houses, transport, health care, education and social services. People go into debt just to survive. The personal result of this onslaught is that we are made to feel that our needs are individual, are material and that we cannot rely on other people to help. This dreadful isolation is the price we are really paying. It is vital to the inclusion movement to acknowledge that this isolation is created deliberately to keep us buying things and services. *Micheline Mason, Alliance for Inclusive Education*

There are macro policies that at first sight may seem unconnected with inclusion and mental health but actually are attached to the same thread. They are about creating a sense of qualitative dignity. I particularly commend the notion of a citizen's income, an income paid as of right to everybody. Now if you want to do this the only practical way is to look at ecological tax reform, through shifting the whole basis of taxation off income and VAT – after all creating income and creating value are good things, so why tax them – onto things like pollution and the use of non-renewable resources. That might seem a long way from the starting point of this Inquiry, but the thing about inclusion is that it's about following threads, and when you do you end up in some surprising places. *Perry Walker, New Economics Foundation*

Several witnesses spoke of the need for befrienders and bridge-builders in creating access to everyday activities for mental health service users. This work needs to be triggered and supported by mental health services themselves, and as such is dealt with mainly in the following section 3.2, but it is worth mentioning here the range of potential allies in the community:

At Community Connections in Nottingham we formed a network of people working for inclusion, particularly bridge-builders. A bridge-builder in the local Museum has been a strong ally, so that users for example always attend the big exhibition launches and drink white wine with the sheriff. We now have 75 agencies in Nottingham that have said yes to welcoming people with serious long-term mental health needs. These agencies are as varied as a residential care home and a police stables. What we have found in Nottingham is that we are actually surrounded by allies in the move for inclusion. Staff at Community Connections delivered mental health training to over 400 members of the public – and we found experts in inclusion just around the corner, disguised as teachers, as parents of children with disabilities, as shopkeepers. We found that if we ask individuals to open up, to include others, then – not always, but often – people will say, 'Yes, we'll welcome people, we'll support them, we'll offer them opportunities.' *Peter Bates, National Development Team*

Finally, several witnesses drew attention to the need for mental health service users to have equal access to general health services:

One thing our volunteer befrienders have been able to do is help the clients – people from minority ethnic groups with long-term mental health problems – to access general health services, their GP for example. The befrienders can provide support, finding out what primary care services are available, helping with language difficulties, giving people more confidence to go and ask for what they need from health services, home care services and so on. *Marilyn Bryan, Awetu Black Mental Health Project*

In the NHS Wales Equality Unit we are actively looking at how people access health services. We have an enormous agenda, but we are working towards widening the definition of equality to include all groups receiving services. We are trying to move away from the 'pigeonhole' approach to equality, where you 'do gender', you 'do race' and so on. We are moving towards a more inclusive approach. And we want to be sure that approach includes the needs of people with mental health problems. We are looking carefully at the information we provide about our services – obviously we need to pay attention to being accessible to people who don't have English as their first language – but also we need to pay attention to the style of our language, to make it less jargon-ridden and excluding. We also need to make sure we give the same messages –

sometimes we end up being excluding because you have medical professionals saying one thing, social services something else and the voluntary sector yet another thing. Finally, we need to get the people who use the services more involved in the policy and planning processes. *Voirrey Manson, NHS Equality Unit*

Mental health services

While they cannot effect social inclusion on their own – legal reform, public education and local community initiatives also need to come into play – mental health services need to be the standard-bearers. The mental health world cannot blame 'the community', 'the law' or 'the media' for promoting discrimination and exclusion if it is engaged in the same thing itself. Once the initial commitment and vision are there, it seems the mechanisms needed to effect inclusion are already available to service providers – it's choosing to look for them that is the key.

Employment and training

The National Health Service has a potentially transformative role to play in the area of mental health and employment. Recent years have seen some policies that do not promote inclusion – notably the Clothier Report[1] and recommendations arising from it – but have also seen some steps towards new ways of supporting users, new employment practices, 'joined-up' thinking and working with external agencies:

Many health providers would challenge the idea that they have any role in employment issues. At Lewisham and Guy's NHS Trust we feel that without our input as mental health service providers, and changing the way we do things, people will be denied opportunities that significantly impact on their mental health. This is particularly the case for people with severe and enduring mental health problems. There are three main areas we must address: our own employment practice, i.e. people with mental health problems as our employees; maximising opportunities within the community, i.e. supporting other agencies to provide opportunities appropriate to people with mental health problems; and promoting access to these opportunities, i.e. how we support

1   *The Clothier Report (1994) was the result of an inquiry into the killings of child patients by nurse Beverley Allitt. Its recommendations included mental health screening of nurses. In consequence there have been reports of discriminatory employment practices and a climate in which it is risky for nurses to seek psychological help when they need it, or be open about their past experience of mental distress.*

people to make use of them. *Tony Coggins, Lewisham and Guy's Mental Health Trust*

What's been set up at South West London and St George's Mental Health Trust is a threefold programme. First we offer supported employment to people who have experienced serious mental health problems. That means we employ support workers who help people in the process of applying for jobs – filling in forms, preparing for interviews and so on. Those workers then also carry on with support work once the person is in post. So far we have filled over 30 posts – and these are ordinary jobs within the trust, we didn't invent jobs.

Second, we set up a parallel volunteer programme. This is aimed at helping people who have never had experience of work to gain some voluntary experience, as a stepping-stone. So far we have employed 34 volunteers, and 40 per cent of them have gone on into open employment, either within the Trust or outside.

Third, we have looked at the practices the Trust uses in all its employment. We employ 1,200 people, and we have developed a charter which states that in all client contact and clinical contact the personal experience of mental health problems is a desirable characteristic. We've also changed our equal opportunities statement explicitly to encourage applications from people who have experienced mental health problems. Since then 13 per cent of our applicants have experience of mental health problems, and 9 per cent of the people we have employed. We have a long way to go, but we have found that we have taken on very good people at all levels of the Trust – including senior managers, psychiatrists and catering personnel – who've experienced mental health problems. *Rachel Perkins, South West London and St George's Mental Health NHS Trust*

Turning services outwards

Promoting inclusion means turning mental health services outwards towards the community. Berating communities for being prejudiced and excluding will have a negligible effect if services are colluding in the exclusion. Service providers who have successfully countered nimby campaigns found that the best results were achieved by working with the local community, recognising people's fears, and supporting users themselves in doing education and outreach work:

Some neighbours are hostile to long-stay patients moving into their street. Once the facility is established the opposition dies down as people realise the new residents are quiet and orderly, but this does not mean the new neighbours make any effort to get to know the residents. However, we found that a focused education campaign in a street in which a sheltered home was being established was successful in reducing locals' fears. In the end a number of them visited the new residents and established social relationships with them. *Julian Leff, Institute of Psychiatry*

Other witnesses also commented on the importance of mental health services seeking out and nurturing community links:

Forging community links, for example with local residents' associations and community projects, as well as the local arts council, really helped us. *South Bedfordshire Community Health Care Trust (written evidence)*

As a community liaison officer for North West London Mental Health Trust my remit was to counter opposition to a new home, set up as part of the Shenley Hospital resettlement project. The skills needed to counteract such prejudice are those of PR and marketing, rather than those needed to manage psychiatric or welfare services. We planned a campaign on conventional PR lines and it worked. We have established a community liaison group, with some of the main objectors as members, and a 'Friends of' volunteer group. We received excellent press coverage, and the residents moved in without problems. *Judy Wurr (written evidence)*

It is our view that a programme of community dialogue and education must be at the centre of any mental health strategy. Money needs to be spent to help change attitudes amongst non-service-users, not just on resources for users. *Community Housing and Therapy (written evidence)*

As a mental health service provider it is very easy to become introspective and hide behind the walls of the project. This happened to us at the Stress Centre, and it was recognised as a problem because it reinforced the idea to people 'outside' that mental health problems should be hidden away. In order to tackle this the new post of development and outreach worker was created to increase the profile of the centre, encourage members to take up opportunities in the community and to feed back to outside service providers any discriminatory practices users experienced. The users themselves have undertaken a lot of this outreach work, making connections with the wider community, including making a video about their experiences that has been used in training psychiatrists and other professionals. We also offer relaxation classes to other projects and groups, led by a worker and a user at the centre. *Pilton Outreach Project (written evidence)*

This evidence is backed up by previous research on nimbyism, which consistently shows that local familiarisation with service users can tap a pool of goodwill and reduce rejections of people with mental health problems (Wolff *et al.* 1996). The conclusion is that real inclusion work, while it might start with neighbouring, must look further:

I think inclusion means a lot more than neighbouring. Many mental health workers, particularly in supported housing, are expending a lot of energy trying to get people to be good neighbours. Now neighbouring is good, but most of us get to know people through our work, through our leisure interests and so on. I don't count my best friends as the people I live a minute's walk from. We need to look at people's whole lives – leisure, work, education – all those life domains need supportive bridge-building work to reconnect mental health service users with their communities of choice.

When statutory and voluntary mental health services at last begin to realise that users are citizens first, friends and loved ones second, employees and enthusiasts third, and users of mental health services only fourth or fifth, then all our imprisoning laws and relationships change. Then users make real friends with a neighbour, fall in love at work, or fall out with the barman at the local pub. *Peter Bates, National Development Team*

Witnesses working in community outreach posts in mental health organisations spoke of opening up new ways of looking at problems, of an attitude shift that highlighted the gaps in current approaches, but showed the way forward as well:

Social services in Coventry recognised a need for developing opportunities in the community for people with mental health problems, specifically within education and leisure. I took up the post of mental health access officer two years ago, and was immediately hit by the gaps in the services. I started looking at other areas, at employment and volunteering particularly, and then a new set of issues was thrown up – transport, benefits, gaps in awareness both within and outside mental health services. Moving people into the community fundamentally challenges traditional practice, because it is empowerment, moving on, fulfilling potential – as opposed to containment. There hadn't been a post like mine before, so the interconnectedness of all these problems had not really come to light. But it's meant that I can get involved across the board, so I work with the NHS, with voluntary organisations like Mind, with local education services, with local leisure services. *Jan Turnbull, Coventry Social Services*

Most mental health workers I come across are unaware of the possibilities in inclusion work. They haven't read the literature, haven't heard a strategist, haven't seen projects where inclusion in community life is the aim. This is a serious gulf. Even where there are projects, they tend to be working with one client group – for example a project might be working with people with learning disabilities only, so the ideas fail to trickle through to mental health. Or a project might be focused entirely on getting people into waged employment – excellent goal – but people who need support in taking up leisure activities in the community are not being served. Or the project might only have one strategy – say systematic instruction to support people in getting into work. Fine, works for some people, but not everyone needs a coach. While these individual strategies are vital, there is a whole range of other areas of life that needs to be incorporated. The absolute key to inclusion work is that by definition it cannot be done with a one-size-fits-all mentality. *Peter Bates, National Development Team*

Picking up on the inappropriateness of one-size-fits-all, several witnesses drew attention to the need for culturally specific and ethnically sensitive work as being axiomatic to inclusive services. Black and minority ethnic voluntary groups are at the forefront of promoting the kind of 'cross-boundary' services many witnesses say are needed, services that do not pigeonhole mental health, welfare, employment and so on as issues to be dealt with in isolation:

> There is a tendency not to join together some of the issues that face black people and then understand how that has an overall impact on services. Recently, however, we've pinpointed areas where services are working effectively. These services tend to be set up to work with specific communities, Asian or Caribbean, or other groups. These services also tend to be run by black voluntary organisations and black people are involved in the service process, managing and delivering.
>
> A lot of black voluntary organisations fit into that model, so if you go to the Black Resource Centre in Dudley Road in Birmingham, although it was originally set up to provide services to old people, now they have daycare for children, a mental health support group – the holistic approach is very much in evidence.
>
> But we do need a great shift in attitude here from mainstream providers across health and social services. However well black voluntary groups do they can never provide all the services needed, it's only going to be when mainstream services change the way they work that we will move on. *Jabeer Butt, Race Equality Unit*

> We work specifically with black and minority ethnic people with enduring mental health problems. We have a befriending service which works in tandem with the local mental health teams and looks to help clients access the whole range of services: housing support, welfare and benefits advice, mental health advocacy, employment opportunities, general health care services. We are the only project of its kind currently in Wales and our effectiveness depends completely on our inter-agency working. *Marilyn Bryan, Awetu Black Mental Health Project*

> We need to recognise the specific needs of Irish people in Britain. We need to provide support for families and carers of people with mental health problems; we need a recognition from the doctors and other health professionals that they need to see and to support their client in their family/cultural environment. *Kilburn Irish Youth Project (written evidence)*

The evident inability of services to respond appropriately to clients from minority ethnic communities is in some regards paralleled by the breakdowns and gaps in services for people referred to as having a 'dual diagnosis'. The very existence of this term is testament to the failure of services driven by diagnosis rather than support needs. (It is also a term that causes some confusion as it is applied both to people with co-existing learning disabilities and mental health problems, and to people with co-existing drug difficulties and mental health problems.)

To some extent the term dual diagnosis is now being replaced by the term complex needs, which is a nod in the direction of more client-focused models, but is still problematic in its implication that people who don't have more than one official diagnosis have 'simple needs'. If there is one theme underlying the whole of the evidence received by the Panel, it is that everyone has 'complex needs', and that trying to legislate away those complexities by giving people simple diagnostic labels is a process that in itself creates social exclusion.

It is recognised that social exclusion can often result in people coming into contact with the police and the criminal justice system, and witnesses involved in mental health work in this area once more emphasised the multi-agency approach needed if clients were to be given meaningful help:

> Revolving Doors focuses on the specific links between mental health and criminal justice. We aim to provide support to mentally vulnerable people at the point of arrest. We identified a group of people, known to local health and social services, who were coming into contact with the police over minor offences – drunk and disorderly, breach of the peace and so on. They were mainly men, in their early thirties, and they all have multiple problems. As well as having mental health problems they have drug or alcohol problems, housing difficulties, financial and employment difficulties.
>
> We provide support at the point of arrest. This is important because they are minor offenders who tend to be cautioned and released, so often the point of arrest is the only time social care agencies can get in contact with these clients. Our principal aim then is to improve the links between social care services and these clients, and in every case a multi-agency approach is crucial to the project.
>
> There are three key principles to our work. First, flexibility; things like visiting people in their own homes rather than insisting

on appointments in clinics or offices. We do a lot of home visits, or if people prefer we meet them in local cafés. Second, persistence; we don't adopt the 'three missed appointments and the case is closed' approach. We keep plugging away until we make an initial contact, find out if there is anything we can do, and try and establish a relationship. Third, and this follows on from the other two, is that this is a time- and resource-intensive approach. To do that we restrict the size of our caseloads to a maximum of 15 ongoing cases per worker. *Toby Seddon, Revolving Doors Agency*

Evidence submitted to the Inquiry by the Metropolitan Police Service closely echoed the above points:

It is essential that there is clear agreement between local agencies about protocols for dealing with people with mental health problems when they come into contact with the police. For example Divisions within the London Borough of Westminster have a forensic community psychiatric nurse on call. This enables assessment and diversion of people with mental health problems close to the point of arrest and has proved successful in linking in with local community provisions. In addition to our work with Revolving Doors [above], we are involved in partnership work with Working Together for Mental Health in Southwark, a group that brings together housing, social services, health services and police to provide a practical response, using named workers and regular liaison meetings, to council tenants experiencing mental health problems. We also work with the Charing Cross Homeless Person's Unit, which is working towards developing a unified approach to homelessness, incorporating housing support, general health and mental health support. *Metropolitan Police Service (written evidence)*

Children and young people also suffer from the lack of appropriate services available to them at crucial points in their lives. The Government's Social Exclusion Unit has focused on children and young people in its first wave of work (see section 3.1 p. 68), and it is vital that mental health support is properly integrated into all new initiatives. Witnesses specifically called for the recognition of the need for increased community-based provision for young people's mental health, and for a focus on prevention as well as appropriate treatments. There was concern that young people were inappropriately sucked into mental health services that could not offer them help, and at that point could be tipped into an adult psychiatric 'career', which different interventions could have avoided:

> We need more places where young people in distress can meet their peers, talk to people with similar experiences, hear about the possibilities of getting better, of moving on. We need to look at people aged 14–25 and attempt to construct services that enable them to grow up at their own pace, to find their own understanding of themselves.
>
> And I am afraid the fact that welfare to work increasingly appears to be the only show in town in terms of funding for young people's agencies is very unfortunate in our view. We need to make some provision for helping young people whose lifestyle is making it difficult for them to concentrate on work or training but who are not 'on the sick'. There is no point in putting such pressure on these young people that they are precipitated into the psychiatric system.
>
> It is our experience that there is widespread support from within local communities for working with young people. At 42nd Street our active and growing team of volunteers attests to this. We believe many communities want to ensure better services for young people – there is particularly striking evidence from black communities about their concern about what is happening to their young people and what they can do to change it. *Alistair Cox, 42nd Street*

Once again, the evidence suggested that problems could only be addressed through a shift in perception, a move away from the 'not-until-a-crisis' approach and recognition of the mental health support lying untapped in local communities:

> Traditional services have ghettoised users. They have severed their links with other citizens. Mental health services need a new vision. We need to focus on inclusion, not exclusion; on building welcoming communities, rather than looking for problems; we need to focus on friendships rather than homicides. *Peter Bates, National Development Team*

3.3 **Summary and conclusions**

The Panel heard compelling evidence that inclusion work is already going on, and, most importantly, is getting results. Many witnesses commented on how important it was that the Inquiry gave them the opportunity to make known good examples of such work, either on their own behalf or others in the field. Contrary to what might perhaps have been expected, given the evidence of exclusion the Panel heard, people working for inclusion have found they are often 'pushing against an open door' – once the real issues are understood, it is very possible to find allies in the community and to get all parties working for the same end.

Mental health and social inclusion – what works and what's needed

Employment

- Employers take the mental wellbeing of their employees very seriously. Many large employers already have in place, for example, counselling services or peer counselling systems. Larger employers are also very aware of their obligations under the Disability Discrimination Act (DDA). They have explicitly asked for more guidance on how to translate support for good practice in mental health into action in the workplace.

- A key area of reform in the DDA in relation to employment practice is to restrict employers' ability to discriminate prior to appointment – this would involve a restriction on the questions regarding medical histories an employer is allowed to ask on application forms.

- Issues of confidentiality and disclosure within the workplace are vexed for both employers and employees. A comprehensive set of guidelines for both parties on how best to handle sensitive health information is needed. The basic premise on which these guidelines need to be founded is that information is on a 'need-to-know' basis, focused on practical requirements in the workplace, rather than personal information about diagnosis or history.

- Very often, reasonable adjustments in the workplace in relation to mental health are positive all round. All employees have mental health needs, and measures to support people who may have particular problems will benefit all.

- The National Health Service can play a leading role with regard to employment and mental health via its own employment practice. There are already some pioneering and successful models of good practice within the NHS, which need to be disseminated and further built upon.

- Existing benefit regulations are an impediment to inclusive employment. There have been some beneficial reforms, but further changes are needed, for example making the testing of incapacity for work less threatening, allowing people with limited capacity to work to earn more while receiving benefits, and ensuring that housing costs do not prevent people from earning. These would go a long way towards promoting equality of employment opportunity for people with mental health problems.
- Both employers and mental health service providers called for the establishment of a national mental health and employment body. A focal agency, working in partnership with employers and with all parts of the mental health services, will greatly enhance inclusion within employment. Currently development is patchy and uncoordinated, with mental health service providers acting in isolation and employers and employees not knowing where to go for information and advice.
- Working with employers and understanding their agenda is a prerequisite to effective change. The arguments for providing workplaces that support and promote mental wellbeing are compelling for both employers and employees. Good mental health means good business, and employers need help in achieving this.

Education and training

- In schools, lessons in promoting mental health come from the movement for inclusive education. Models of giving control back to service users – in this case children – and promoting inclusion already exist. They have a huge contribution to make towards children's mental health.
- Disability and inclusion work in further and higher education has tended thus far to focus on physical barriers to access. Recent reports in the field, including the Tomlinson report (Further Education Funding Council 1996), have moved the mental health agenda forward by highlighting the under-representation of people with mental health problems in further and higher education. More research and auditing are needed to establish what is already being done and what strategies need to be implemented in the future.
- Creating support systems for people with mental health problems is particularly important in further and higher education because this can often be the point at which people first experience mental health problems.
- Educational institutions need to develop and sustain support services that relate to local health services.

- Some institutions have established 'starter' courses for people with mental health problems, which are geared to students' needs. In terms of inclusion work, these are vital stepping-stones on the way to full inclusion, i.e. enrolment in mainstream education for those who want to do so.
- The particular needs of mature students, part-time students, international students and minority ethnic students must be properly researched. Mental health issues within education are far more diverse than the stereotypical 'exam stress'.
- Much greater co-operation between social services, mental health services and educational bodies is needed, both with regard to mental health promotion/mental illness prevention for existing students, and creating greater access for existing users of mental health services.

Arts and media
- The media have been implicated in worsening discriminatory attitudes towards mental health service users, and thereby directly contributing to social exclusion. Just as the media have been a force for exclusion, they can be a force for inclusion. Mental health services and service users are becoming strategic in accessing the media – we need to master the art of 'spin'.
- Promoting positive role models – successful/well-known people as well as 'ordinary members of the public' talking about living with mental health problems – has a tremendous power to demystify and destigmatise.
- Pro-active work by service users themselves, and their supporters, in gaining access to the airwaves and giving journalists their side of the story has been very effective.
- Media monitoring has an important part to play. Media organisations are sensitive to readers'/viewers'/listeners' views, and coordinated action to get these views across gets mental health issues onto the media producers' agenda.
- It is increasingly recognised that the arts can play a catalytic role in promoting social inclusion, both by virtue of the participative processes involved and the innovative 'products' created. Whether in drama, visual arts, poetry or other forms, artistic product can help audiences to grasp truths about mental health in a non-doctrinaire context.
- While specific arts therapies for mental health problems are an important part of mental health service, once again it is important not to mistake

mid-points for end-points. Art therapies within mental health services can sometimes contribute to feelings of exclusion; putting service users' work on the walls of mental health facilities will not promote inclusion – working to get service users access to arts courses in the local community will.

Daily living: access to goods, services and social networks

- Commercial imperatives can be harnessed to promote inclusion – there is a strong business case for making goods and services available to as wide a range of people as possible. Some service providers may be unaware that their services or the manner in which they are delivered are discriminatory; where service users can draw attention to this, changes and adjustments can follow.

- The Disability Discrimination Act potentially has a large role to play here, with its broad definition of goods and services. Awareness of the legislation needs to be raised amongst all service providers, private, statutory and voluntary, and attention paid to enforcement.

- New ways of selling – particularly those using new technologies such as the internet – can be a great benefit to people with mental health problems. There is scope for mutually beneficial partnership with goods and service providers in promoting these forms of access.

- While commercial imperatives can be harnessed for inclusion, the Inquiry evidence also points to the need to look more searchingly – and imaginatively – at economic processes. In very many cases economic forces drive exclusion; an example often cited is the withdrawal of high-street banks from areas deemed not to be worth the costs of running a local branch. Mental health service users are very vulnerable to these kinds of forces, and the promotion of social firms, LETS schemes and other innovative forms of creating value and exchanging goods and services must be taken seriously by mental health services.

- The National Health Service and local social services need to put their own houses in order by ceasing to exclude mental health service users from general health care and housing and other support services. Equal rights to health and social care are enshrined in Government policy and patients' charters, and covered in some aspects now by the Disability Discrimination Act.

- In areas of social support other than health – most particularly housing – the tendency towards ghettoisation must be countered. To this end generic housing agencies and providers need to be encouraged to take into account the needs of mental health service users in all their housing provision. Only in this way can properly integrated and inclusive environments be fostered. There is still a need for specialist supported housing, but it must not take the place of genuinely inclusive practice by non-specialist providers.

- The process of 'bridge-building', pioneered for example by Community Connections in Nottingham, can transform mental health service users' access to community life. Health and social services need to turn outwards, so that bridge-builders go out into the community, talk to people – gym managers, shopkeepers, teachers and lecturers, commercial employers, charities, the police, pub landlords – and offer advice and training in the issues and problems facing mental health service users in the community. This work reveals a network of unexpected allies and experts in the work of social inclusion.

Mental health services

- Mental health services must realise their key role in fostering inclusion for users. While mental health services cannot do it alone, no other agency can do it without them.
- Community development activities and partnerships that stretch beyond health and social services alone are central to mental health work. This has profound implications for how services are designed and run.
- A key factor in the reconfiguration of services to promote inclusion is to look at providing mental health services in non-mental health settings. This move acknowledges both the 'holistic' nature of mental health problems and care, and also deconstructs the stigma associated with services designated as 'only for mental health problems'. The onus is on service providers to begin to think in a more holistic way.
- Services stand to gain within their own existing terms; local work to improve social inclusion for people with mental health problems has been shown to bring demonstrable health gain and contribute significantly to 'clinical effectiveness'.
- Some highly effective work is beginning to be done in the field of employment for mental health service users. Mental health trusts are seeking collaboration with local employment agencies – Employment Services, Training and Enterprise Councils, Economic Development Units and so on – as well as other local statutory agencies, and are effectively promoting employment for users. A few trusts are pioneering the employment of mental health service users within their own ranks – with excellent results.

- Successful countering of nimbyism by some services has shown the effectiveness of good 'marketing skills' – pro-active use of local media, full partnership with service users in education and familiarisation programmes, and ongoing work in fostering and expanding links with local community life.
- Inclusion work by definition repudiates the 'one-size-fits-all' approach of traditional health and social services. Particular attention must be paid to the needs of minority ethnic service users, who can experience multiple and compound exclusions because of racist discrimination. A number of services set up by and for minority ethnic groups have been pioneering in their holistic approach to support provision.
- Similarly, service users described as having a 'dual diagnosis' or 'complex needs' stand to benefit from services switching from a diagnosis/service- or even needs-driven model to one in which an individual's requirements are seen in relation to his/her engagement with wider communities.
- Work with people with mental health problems who come into contact with the police has shown that by determined inter-agency working and time- and resource-intensive approaches, individuals who have become 'disengaged' with services that have not previously addressed their needs can be offered effective support.
- Young people, in particular those aged 14–25, have been shown to experience particular difficulty with mental health services, contact with which many experience as a contributory factor to their exclusion. Again, careful work across different 'life domains' – housing, education, general health, employment/training, family support – can be instrumental in allowing young people the time to find their feet. Such interventions can save years of distress – costly to the individual, to services and to the wider community – later on.
- The evidence has shown that basic forms of care, support and attention are valued very highly by service users. Yet the people within mental health services who do most of this daily care work – such as care assistants – are denied the acknowledgement and status their work deserves. Health and social care services need to look at ways of formally raising the status of such care work. Increasing the status of care workers in turn increases the status of those cared for, and thus creates another momentum towards inclusion.
- The first steps in inclusion work can seem to uncover insurmountable obstacles. But as the interconnectedness of problems is revealed, so new

ways of working – the interconnectedness of solutions – also appear. Mental health services have a key and privileged role to play in helping to create a more inclusive society.

Conclusions

This Government has declared reducing social exclusion in Britain to be one of its central aims, and has pointed to the necessity of multi-agency working to achieve it. At the same time, mental health service users' experience of pervasive and sometimes brutal social exclusion is forcing mental health service providers to look beyond their traditional service boundaries. These trends together can generate a real momentum for work in the field of social exclusion and mental health. This work can involve not only addressing the needs of current and future mental health service users, but also looking more broadly at the mental health component of *all* inclusion work.

The evidence presented to this Inquiry revealed three main foundations on which to build effective inclusion work for people with mental health problems:

- local initiatives driven by mental health services in full and co-operative partnerships with a whole spectrum of local agencies – private, statutory and voluntary;
- legislative and policy reform at Government level, with consistent and complementary policies across Government Departments;
- public education and mental health promotion.

Within the mental health services, it is important that inclusion work goes hand in glove with improved core mental health services. Twenty-four hour, accessible and safe services and adequate residential provision must be in place. But at the same time services must work to support service users in gaining access to their 'communities of choice'. The key is to create effective specialist services while at the same time giving priority to local partnerships beyond health and social services alone. Collaboration with a whole range of local agencies needs to be at the heart of mental health services, not an extra, bolted-on to rehabilitation services and divorced from clinical work.

This has profound implications for how services are judged. As ideas about inclusion begin to permeate all areas of social policy, there is an opportunity to build research findings on successful inclusion work into the evidence base for all mental health services, so that effectiveness and quality standards move beyond simply measuring symptom reduction.

Broader social policy reform is needed to complement the work of mental health services. These are currently thwarted by policies within the benefits, welfare and employment fields that obstruct inclusion work rather than supporting it (see Chapter 4 for specific policy recommendations regarding welfare and employment reform). The Department of Education and Employment has a key role to play, for example, in setting targets for health authorities, employment services and local employers to provide enhanced opportunities in work and training for people with mental health problems. Benefit reform is essential. The Department of Health also needs to produce complementary policies that recognise the full needs of people with mental health problems by emphasising the importance of rehabilitation and actions for inclusion. The National Service Framework for Mental Health and Local Health Improvement Plans, for example, offer valuable opportunities to ensure better collaborative work between health and local authorities. The Panel welcomed the emphasis in the public health White Paper *Saving Lives Our Healthier Nation* (DoH 1999) on 'integrated' action to tackle mental health, and the intention to ensure that 'mental health is regarded as a key outcome of each strand of the Government's agenda'. However, a greater emphasis on the roles and responsibilities of local authorities, and on the active tackling of discrimination and exclusionary attitudes, will be needed if truly 'integrated action' is to be effected.

The Inquiry evidence has shown legal reform to be key. The Disability Discrimination Act had a high profile in the evidence to the Inquiry, and many witnesses pointed to its limitations (see recommendations in Chapter 4 on specific areas of reform). Nonetheless it is unarguable that such a law is crucial in providing a benchmark for society, a signal that discrimination is unacceptable and a kind of searchlight that can be used to reveal exclusionary practices previously unacknowledged or simply unknown to the broader public. A Disability Rights Commission must follow. In addition, the incorporation of the European Convention on Human Rights into UK law provides a fresh opportunity to win popular support for human rights – including those of mental health service users.

Unfortunately, recent and proposed law reform is not all driving towards a vision of a fair and inclusive society. Current proposals for the amendment of the Mental Health Act 1983, as well as proposals from the Home Office relating to preventive detention for those diagnosed with personality disorder, have given many mental health agencies and civil rights groups serious cause for concern. An ethical schism is revealed by these conflicting directions in legislative reform. If the Government's desire to promote social inclusion is to be more than rhetoric, then it must resist the temptation to scapegoat people with mental health problems, who are already experiencing some of the worst social exclusion of any group. Partial inclusion is no inclusion at all.

Public education about mental health problems, and mental health promotion, need to be given a much higher profile than they have in the past. Witnesses to the Inquiry returned again and again to the effects of mass media on public perceptions of people with mental health problems. There is a need for sustained and strategic initiatives, initiatives that set out to change hearts and minds, to tackle the stigma currently attached to mental health service users. Mental health agencies across the statutory, voluntary and private sectors have an obligation to initiate and support this work, and accurate and consistent monitoring of their effect is fundamental to their ongoing impact. The creation of the Health Development Agency, with its emphasis on a strong research base for efficacy in health promotion, including mental health promotion, is a very welcome step (DoH 1999). Also welcome is the promise in the public health White Paper (DoH 1999) of 'national public education campaigns' for use in a wide range of settings, including schools, workplaces and prisons. These campaigns, as well as their stated aims of enhancing social support and coping strategies and tackling bullying, must address the extreme stigma currently attached to mental ill-health. The views and experiences of those with mental health problems will be essential components if these campaigns are to have an effect on existing social exclusion.

New theories of social exclusion are crystallising the understanding that mental health underlies all processes of exclusion/inclusion, both in cause and effect. Until recently, there had been resistance to the idea that deprivation, or exclusion, has a damaging psychological impact. As the Inquiry evidence so vividly illustrates, and as summarised in Figure 1 (p. 46), mental health problems can lead to almost every form of social exclusion, and every form of social exclusion has a potentially negative effect on mental health. How individuals and communities 'feel' is therefore a critical factor in social capital (see p. 64). As one commentator has put it: 'Mental health underpins all health and wellbeing. It influences how we think and feel, how we interpret events, our capacity to communicate and to form and sustain relationships. Mental health also affects our ability to cope with change and trauma. In essence, mental wellbeing underpins social functioning and productivity' (Friedli 1999).

The conclusion from this new appreciation of the place of mental health in the processes of social exclusion is profound and far-reaching: we need to look at planning, policies and services from the perspective of their impact on mental health. This is a vast and potentially overwhelming objective, and clearly beyond mental health services, which have neither the resources nor necessarily the inclination to involve themselves in every programme to improve people's lives. But it does mean that as the rafts of social inclusion programmes and initiatives are developed, mental health commissioners and providers need actively to identify where mental health expertise will add value.

Finally, all the initiatives promoting social inclusion for people with mental health problems will fail unless they ensure the active and influential participation of service users. Again, bolt-on extras and token gestures will not do. The experts in exclusion are the people who experience it, and they too are the people who – given genuine access to and influence over policy and planning processes – will ultimately make social inclusion for all an achievable goal.

CHAPTER 4

'From exclusion to cohesion':

the Inquiry's recommendations

4.1 Recommendations for national policy

National policy – the Social Exclusion Unit

The Inquiry evidence confirms that people with mental health problems are amongst the most seriously and systematically excluded groups in British society. The exclusion needs to be tackled at national policy level by a number of Government Departments in addition to the Department of Health. The Panel therefore recommends that:

- the Social Exclusion Unit should review urgently Government policy as it affects the social exclusion of people with mental health problems. As a senior Government Unit with a remit across Departments, the SEU is ideally placed to take responsibility for the inter-departmental implementation of the recommendations detailed below.

National policy – mental health audits

The Panel welcomed the promise in the recent public health White Paper *Saving Lives: Our Healthier Nation* (DoH 1999) to 'ensure that mental health is regarded as a key outcome of each strand of the Government's agenda to promote social inclusion – from Sure Start to Better Government for Older People, from the Rough Sleepers Initiative the Welfare to Work programme, and across the range of local initiatives'. The Panel further recommends that:

- the impact on mental health of all new social policies and initiatives should be a key determinant in assessing their viability and effectiveness.

- Government, research and academic bodies should look at developing sensitive measures of mental wellbeing and mental ill-health as a fundamental part of the social inclusion/exclusion model. These measures take particular account of ethnic and cultural diversity;

- the Government ensures that the performance indicators included in the National Service Framework for Mental Health reflect issues of life quality that have been shown to be important to service users, rather than solely clinical issues such as symptom reduction. An awareness of ethnic and cultural differences must inform all measures of life quality.

National policy – the Disability Rights Commission

The Panel warmly welcomes the Government's setting up of the Disability Rights Commission. The backing of the Commission with strong legislative powers, adequate resources and the full integration of mental health issues into the disability agenda will promise real and concrete improvements in the lives of people with mental health problems.

The Panel recommends that:

- the Government ensures that the Disability Rights Commission takes a pro-active approach to enforcement of anti-discrimination law;

- at least one of the Disability Rights Commissioners appointed to the Commission should have experience of mental health problems;

- the Chair of the Disability Rights Commission ensures that:
    - all Commissioners and staff receive training in mental health issues and in race and cultural awareness
    - the needs of people with mental health problems are reflected in the Commission's programme of work
    - mechanisms are established to involve users of mental health services from all sections of the community in the Commission's work
    - the reduction of social exclusion is used as one of the evaluation criteria for the Commission's work;

- the Disability Rights Commission makes a strong and explicit commitment to raise awareness of the relevance of the Disability Discrimination Act (DDA) to people with mental health problems amongst all goods and service providers – private, statutory and voluntary;

- the Disability Rights Commission establishes strong links with the Mental Health Act Commission, the Commission for Racial Equality and the Equal Opportunities Commission.

National policy – employment

The Panel welcomes the Government's efforts to remove barriers to employment for people with disabilities, including mental health problems. The Inquiry evidence shows that many people with mental health problems want to work and are able to work. Support for people with mental health problems must go hand in hand with support for employers in how to deal with mental health issues in the workplace. Anomalies in the benefits system that put barriers in the way of those attempting to work must be addressed.

In addition, in its welfare to work policies the Government must ensure that it does not give the impression that people are valued only for their economic contribution. Whether in 'spin', Benefits Agency literature or the operation of the welfare system, the Government's messages should be assessed on their impact on people striving to survive and improve their quality of life against a background of mental health problems.

The Panel recommends that:

- the Government or appropriate executive agencies introduce quality standards for providers of supported employment services. Mental health service users must get a good deal from employment schemes, and purchasers of supported employment services must have a basis on which to judge them. Setting and assessing quality standards must involve service users;

- the Government ensures that mental health service users and disabled people have fair access to personal adviser posts and other key roles within welfare reform. They should consider specifying a proportion of personal adviser posts where direct experience of mental distress or disability is an essential criterion for the job;

- training of staff and monitoring of the service ensures that ONE and New Deal (see Glossary) personal advisers respect clients' own assessment of their needs and their strategies for recovery and moving towards work;

- medical tests for incapacity for work should not be repeated unnecessarily or too frequently – people receiving incapacity-related benefits should be encouraged to take up activities that are meaningful without jeopardising their benefits at every stage of their journey towards work;

- further benefit reforms to 'make work pay' and overcome the barriers for people with mental health problems – in particular in relation to help with housing costs – are implemented. The steep taper in Housing Benefit withdrawal, delays in reassessment and payment of Housing Benefit, and the restriction of help with mortgage repayments to people on Income Support, are major barriers to work for those who cannot work full-time and are not confident of sustaining work;

- some welfare to work resources be directed towards support for job creation through social firms, self-employment and co-operatives. This support should include enterprises run by and for people from minority ethnic communities;

- in order to tackle discrimination within the workplace, the Disability Rights Commission should, in partnership with Government agencies, mental health and business organisations, put into action a concerted drive to disseminate mental health information to employers. The aim should be for every employer to know:
    - that disability discrimination applies to mental distress
    - that mental health adjustments can be easy and low cost
    - where to get more information and support;

- the Disability Rights Commission should disseminate guidance that combines the legal obligations around confidentiality of personal information with advice at a more personal level on how to tackle issues of confidentiality and disclosure. This needs the involvement of mental health service users to ensure that the full implications of disclosure, and experience of what is and what is not helpful, inform the guidance;

- the Department of Health and NHS Executive should encourage the employment of mental health service users in the NHS, providing guidance to trusts on fair recruitment and retention and on ways of making adjustments. This could turn around the defensive and unfair recruitment practices reported in the wake of the Clothier Report. There is a rich source of expertise to tap among user-workers in mental health services.

National policy – education and training

The Panel noted a low level of awareness of mental health issues generally within higher and further education. (Although there are honourable exceptions, some of which are highlighted in the evidence.)

The barriers between educational bodies and mental health services seemed particularly impermeable, and a joint lead at national policy level from the Department for Education and Employment and the Department of Health is sorely needed if people with mental health problems are to exercise their right to access education.

The Panel recommends that:

- the Department for Education and Employment supports further research and auditing of inclusion work relating to mental health in further and higher education;

- the Government reforms funding and benefit arrangements to enable students with mental health difficulties to move between full- and part-time study as their health permits;

- the Government maintains the flexibility in the benefits system that allows people on incapacity-related benefits to study up to full time;

- personal advisers in the New Deal and ONE pilots establish high standards of advice to people on incapacity-related benefits, so that they are neither discouraged from taking up courses that would help them, nor do they lose benefit as a result of taking up courses. Guidance for those making decisions on benefit entitlements needs to match up with the advice given to individuals;

- the Government ensures that the new Learning and Skills Framework fully addresses the inclusion of people with mental health problems;

- Funding Councils and other key policy-makers in education should promote successful examples of inclusion work, such as access courses and practical support structures, demonstrating what adjustments are needed in educational institutions;

- quality bodies in education should ensure that the inclusion of students with mental health problems is taken into account in the quality assurance process and reflected in the resulting commendations that institutions receive;

- the Institute for Learning and Teaching, which oversees the accreditation of teacher training in higher education, should include an understanding of the needs of students with mental health difficulties as part of their training requirements.

National policy – mental health promotion, media and the arts

The Panel was very struck by the importance the majority of witnesses attributed to mental health education and to the power of the media. While much damage has been done by ill-informed media reporting about mental health and illness, much good can be derived from using the power of the media to promote inclusion.

The Panel recommends that:

- the Government and national health education and promotional bodies should use the public education resources at their disposal to challenge the public perception of the link between violence and mental ill-health;

- the mental health promotion campaigns outlined in the public health White Paper *Saving Lives: Our Healthier Nation* (DoH 1999) include within their remit not only the promotion of mental wellbeing but an understanding of mental ill-health. 'Stigma-busting' and anti-discrimination education are as important as social support and coping strategies;

- national health promotion and education bodies support the development of user-run groups (including those among the black and minority ethnic communities). Education and training provided by service users has been shown to be most effective in changing attitudes of both professionals and the public;

- the Government provides resources to ensure the effective continuation of groups that challenge inaccurate or bigoted media portrayals of those with mental health problems. Such groups can also train users of the mental health system to use the media effectively and gain a public voice;

- the creation of a national network of arts-based mental health initiatives (including those within the black and minority ethnic communities) is supported, to enable the dissemination of good practice and coordinate uniform and effective working across the country.

4.2 Recommendations for legal reform

Some exclusionary practices are currently actively enshrined in legislation, for example the Representation of the People Act, which the Panel strongly recommends be amended. The Panel is also concerned at the current weaknesses in the Disability Discrimination Act, which disproportionately affect people with mental health problems. The revised Mental Health Act could also become an instrument for further exclusion unless crucial amendments and safeguards are included in the revision.

Legal reform – the Disability Discrimination Act

Legal rights provide an important benchmark of what is acceptable and a means of redress for wronged individuals. Their existence can give an impetus to raising awareness and improving practice. As such, the Disability Discrimination Act (DDA) has played a useful role but its flaws mean that a more effective civil rights law should replace it. Key problems with the DDA are its limited definition of disability that excludes many people with mental health problems, its lack of enforcement mechanisms and – in employment – the difficulties of proving discrimination at the recruitment stage. The Government is establishing a Disability Rights Commission, which will have a key enforcement and educational role (see 4.1 p. 119).

The Panel recommends that:

- the Government enacts comprehensive and enforceable anti-discrimination legislation based on an inclusive definition of disability that will ensure protection for everyone who experiences discrimination due to a disability and that fully includes people with, or regarded as having, mental health problems.

In particular the Panel recommends that such comprehensive anti-discrimination legislation should:

- make it unlawful to ask about medical history before an offer of employment has been made;

- make it unlawful to penalise employees who do not volunteer medical information that is not relevant to their current status and that they have not been asked about;

- include all providers of education and training.

Legal reform – the Mental Health Act

The Panel recommends that the Government's proposed new Mental Health Act should:

- enshrine the principle of non-discrimination on grounds of mental ill-health;

- require Mental Health Tribunals to use the reduction of social exclusion as a criterion in relation to any package of compulsory care;

- require health and social services authorities to state in any package of proposed care (whether compulsory or not) how it will help to reduce social exclusion and promote socially inclusive practice, and to monitor the success of the package against this criterion;

- require the Mental Health Act Commission to include in their annual report to Parliament an assessment of the contribution made by mental health services to reducing the social exclusion experienced by people with mental health problems;

- require the Mental Health Act Commission to work in collaboration with the Disability Rights Commission;

- require monitoring of the use of the Act, including its impact on people from minority ethnic communities.

Legal reform – voting rights and jury service

Certain legislation and policy currently specifically targets people with mental health problems for exclusion. The Panel recommends that:

- the Lord Chancellor's Department should reconsider the exclusion of all people receiving treatment for mental health problems from jury service;

- the Home Office should amend the Representation of the People Act 1983 to enable use of a hospital as a registration address for voting purposes.

4.3 Recommendations for employers and employers' organisations

The Panel heard about the impact of discrimination in and exclusion from the workplace, but also about employers' commitment to taking mental health seriously, and their demand for guidance and support to help them do so. The Panel's vision of inclusive employment is one in which:

- people's abilities are recognised and respected, but work abilities are not taken as the only measure of a person's worth;
- people do not have to be afraid to be open about their experience of mental distress but can still choose privacy;
- people with mental health problems or a history of psychiatric treatment have fair access to mainstream employment;
- there are both enforceable legal rights and the guidance and support to help employers implement them;
- a collective or lead agency is established to promote at national level the employment of people with mental health problems;
- there is space and encouragement for imaginative approaches such as social firms, cooperatives and user-run enterprises.

Legal rights can only be effective if those with duties under the law are given the information, guidance and support they need to fulfil them. Mental health service users will be sold short if the only emphasis is on legal rights. The Inquiry heard that employers wanted to know how to develop and implement policy, and to have their own needs and priorities as employers understood. In particular they wanted guidance on mental health adjustments and handling sensitive health information, and to have a single point of contact for these issues. The Panel drew particular attention to the fact that recommendations directed towards employers apply across the private, statutory and voluntary sector, none of which currently can claim a good record in relation to employment of people with mental health problems.

The Panel recommends that:

- employers ensure that they are informed about mental health in order to establish fair practices in line with the Disability Discrimination Act and any subsequent anti-discrimination law, and to improve the health and functioning of their organisation. This means understanding the mental health dimension in policies and practices concerning equal opportunities, work/life balance, fairness at work, dignity at work and flexibility;

● employers should explicitly include people with mental health problems within equal opportunities policies, and seek advice where necessary on how to make this a reality;

● employers should seek to ensure that their working conditions and practices work for and not against employees' mental health – for example clear communication, anti-bullying policies, staff support systems – and that they are prepared to make reasonable adjustments where an employee needs it. Adjustments should always be made in negotiation with the employee, recognising their expertise in their own needs; managers may need training in how to do this;

● employer organisations should disseminate information about mental health, identifying mental distress or mental illness as an equalities issue, so that human resources, occupational health and senior management recognise this as an area they need to know about and that they have, or can access, the resources to tackle it.

4.4 Recommendations for local authorities

The Panel noted the responsibility of local politicians, councillors and planners not to discriminate against any members of the local community. Too often 'nimby' campaigns have the support of local politicians, who should be taking a lead on creating more inclusive local communities, rather than championing exclusion. As well as opposing nimbyism, local authorities can open up local democratic processes to include wider sections of the community, including those with mental health problems.

The Panel recommends that:

● local authorities, through their national associations, develop training modules for elected councillors on mental health and other equality and diversity issues. There should be a requirement for councillors to undertake such training within a certain period of being elected;

● local authorities open up local community planning and policy to the local community itself, for example using models such as citizens' juries. Combating exclusion involves investing in work to develop the capacity of the community to solve its own problems – by working with community leaders, neighbourhood groups, religious organisations and so on;

● local authorities engage existing voluntary and community organisations, including those from the black and minority ethnic communities, as partners in planning strategy;

● local authorities ensure that the concept of 'best value' used in assessing the services they provide includes the criterion of increasing social inclusion;

● local authorities examine and, where appropriate, support the possible use of LETS schemes in their area to reduce social exclusion.

4.5 **Recommendations for general goods and service providers**

The Inquiry uncovered a woeful lack of knowledge about mental health amongst many providers of general goods and services. Public education about mental health problems has a key role to play here, but the new Disability Rights Commission, and the provisions of any new anti-discrimination law, must look at ways to encourage people who supply goods and services to the public to understand the needs of those with mental health problems.

The Panel recommends that:

● all goods and service providers, in the statutory, voluntary and commercial sector, should be encouraged to consider different ways of providing their services (such as internet shopping) which will make them accessible to a wider range of people. Trade bodies in the manufacturing, retail and service sectors have an important role to play in highlighting the benefits to both suppliers and customers of innovative forms of delivery;

● discussions should take place at national level between representatives of the financial, banking and insurance industries and mental health organisations about ways of reducing the discrimination faced by those with a current or past mental illness diagnosis.

4.6 Recommendations for education and training bodies

The Panel was made aware that the quality of support offered during childhood, adolescence or early adulthood was a key factor determining whether people were excluded later in adult life. Education and training establishments need to be at the forefront of creating mentally healthy and supportive environments for children and for students and trainees.

The Panel recommends that:

- local education authorities promote existing examples of effective inclusion work in schools, and provide support services to enable schools to keep children with particular psychological needs or behavioural issues in the mainstream;

- education and training bodies review their policies, procedures and practices to eliminate or amend those that discriminate against people with mental health problems. In particular, vocational courses, especially nursing and medical professions and those involving work with children, should ensure that they operate fair admissions criteria;

- education and training bodies explicitly recognise students with mental health problems in their equal opportunities statements and policies. They should set out in their general literature what adjustments they may be able to offer, and what kinds of support are available and how to access them;

- education bodies work with students and ex-students with experience of mental distress to run distress awareness events and training across the whole institution, and to develop ideas for support structures;

- education bodies examine course structures and as far as possible make adjustments so that students with intermittent mental health problems can continue studying as and when they are able, and work at their own pace;

- education bodies, especially providers of further and higher education, develop support systems for students with mental health difficulties. These could include:
  - peer support
  - an adviser with whom to discuss learning needs and how to

communicate them to teaching staff
- advocacy to assist students to articulate and assert their needs
- counselling
- e.mail contact
- someone to accompany the student, for example, to help them become confident in negotiating the college/campus or making contact with other students
- access to local mental health services and support groups;

• education bodies address the broader mental health needs of a diverse student population and of the institution as a whole. The specific needs of mature, part-time, international and minority ethnic students should be researched;

• voluntary sector health and mental health organisations make efforts to establish direct links with schools, colleges and universities in their area, with a view to mental health promotion work and providing mental health support services.

4.7 Recommendations for general health and social care services

Local health authorities can have a pivotal role in creating the holistic services necessary to break the cycle of social exclusion. The Panel noted that many recommendations for interagency working are already part of policy objectives for statutory health and social care services, but the mental health dimension has very often been overlooked. Similarly, links between the statutory and voluntary sector are strengthening, but need to go wider and deeper. The Panel also felt that voluntary sector health and social care providers need to make a thorough commitment to tackling exclusion in their own internal policy and practice, as well as in the services they offer.

The Panel recommends that:

• statutory health authorities and voluntary providers look at forging partnerships with mental health specialist services to establish mental health services in non-mental-health settings. This is vital in increasing outreach, decreasing stigma and reflecting a more holistic view of health and social care;

- health authorities use public health reports to map and measure changes in the pattern and degree of social exclusion of different groups within society – including people with mental health problems. Such measurements must also look at the specific experiences of minority ethnic groups;

- the new Public Health Observatories (see Glossary) to be set up in each NHS region (DoH 1999) should have a strong emphasis on mental health and must develop more sensitive measures of mental health and ill-health than suicide rates;

- health authorities set targets for improvements in social inclusion in their Health Improvement Programme and Health Action Zone Plan (if any). Improvements in social inclusion should also be one of the criteria for measuring service effectiveness;

- voluntary sector providers incorporate the promotion of social inclusion into quality measurements across their services, and audit the mental health impact of these services;

- health authorities make links to all local authority departments – not just social services. They need to ensure any Health Improvement Programme is concordant with local regeneration programmes, plans for youth justice, children's services, race action plans, LEA behavioural support plans, education action zones (if any), community care – and more – in order to provide a comprehensive service that works to enhance quality of life rather than response to illness alone;

- voluntary sector health and social care providers strengthen links with local health authorities and social services, and begin to build links with other local statutory bodies, including education, police and criminal justice and equality bodies;

- health authorities work with primary care groups to ensure that community development and regeneration agendas are represented in practices primary care groups (PCGs) and primary care trusts;

- health authorities target primary prevention activities at excluded groups – such as refugees or homeless people – through collaboration with New Deal, Lifelong Learning and other measures to enhance inclusion and improve mental health;

- health authorities and the new Public Health Observatories examine the morbidity and mortality rates for people with long-term mental health problems, and assess whether discrimination is occurring in relation to the delivery of physical health care, including that within primary health care. Codes of practice, training and monitoring to remedy any discrimination must be put in place;

- health authorities engage voluntary and community organisations from all communities as partners in planning strategy. Particularly important is the proper engagement of mental health service users in planning;

- primary care service providers involve local user, voluntary and community groups in their work (including those from the black and minority ethnic communities);

- Healthy Living Centres incorporate measures for ensuring that people with mental health problems are fully included in their work;

- the National Institute for Clinical Effectiveness (NICE) should ensure that improvement in social inclusion and reduction of health inequality is one of the criteria used to judge the effectiveness of interventions in the mental health field;

- the clinical governance framework include targets and performance measures derived from a user-focused perspective; and provides for reliable and relevant monitoring of outcomes.

4.8 Recommendations for mental health services

Social inclusion for service users should be the primary aim of mental health services, across both health and social care. Too narrow a focus on clinical and treatment interventions means that many users feel badly let down by services that should be helping them. The Panel heard evidence of a re-orientation of services in recognition of this need, but developments were piecemeal. The Panel emphasised the need to site mental health services in non-mental-health settings, to make them more accessible, less stigmatised and more holistic in their approach to the causes and cures of mental ill-health.

Mental health services – incorporating social inclusion

The National Service Framework for Mental Health cannot work in isolation from the communities in which services operate and in which service users live their lives. In order to make social inclusion central to mental health care, the Panel recommends that mental health and primary care service providers across the voluntary and statutory sectors should:

- ensure that the experience of exclusion or discrimination is included in all aspects of service assessment, such as the Care Programme Approach, by the use of user-focused assessment tools;

- work in partnership with service users to agree desired outcomes with the aim of ensuring that they have access to roles, relationships and activities in the communities of their choice, and can, as far as possible, live the lives that they choose;

- support local user, voluntary and community groups (including black and minority ethnic groups) to be part of the local service network;

- ensure mental health services are free of discrimination – on grounds including mental health status, ethnicity, age, gender disability, and sexual orientation – through effective equal opportunities policies, monitoring and training;

- equip mental health staff to support service users from all communities in gaining access to social and economic opportunities and in developing strategies to deal with discrimination and how to combat it if they choose;

- employ (possibly jointly with general health services) community liaison/development workers focused on ensuring access for service users to the communities of their choice and developing links with befrienders and bridge-builders within all local communities;

- ensure that users from all communities are involved – through users' forums, joint work with advocacy groups, employing user consultants – in determining measures of quality, outcome and 'best value' and in setting research agendas. This ensures that users' priorities are fully reflected in the evidence base that is used as a backdrop to local strategies, service frameworks and commissioning;

- ensure the availability of 24-hour accessible and safe services and adequate residential provision appropriate to all service users, taking account of ethnic and cultural diversity;

- develop comprehensive community-based provision for young people from all sections of the community;

- ensure that mainstream services take account of the needs of different ethnic groups, and resource culturally-specific provision in the voluntary sector;

- carry out an audit of services available to those with a dual diagnosis/complex needs and identify ways in which these can be better met such as the appointment of workers with links to both services who can act as key workers for individuals with complex needs;

- develop links with the local police service and other criminal justice agencies, and develop appropriate referral policies.

Mental health services – employment

The mental health system was repeatedly criticised during the Inquiry for doing very little to promote users' employment, and indeed as an employer itself it shows no confidence in users' abilities. The Panel found a lot of scope for mental health services to put their own house in order as employers, and to give more priority to users' work needs and aspirations within their treatment and care.

The Panel recommends that:

- mental health organisations with a stake in providing employment information, advice and support services, or in advocating service users' employment interests, should negotiate to establish a collective or lead voice to promote employment for people with mental health problems more;

- mental health service providers in both statutory and voluntary sectors take a lead as employers by valuing the contribution users bring to mental health work and encouraging their appointment. For example
  - positively welcome applications from users and ex-users of mental health services
  - set targets for their employment at all levels of the organisation

- consider developing employment projects, like that at South West London and St George's Mental Health NHS Trust, which employs and supports people with serious mental health problems in a range of clinical posts;

● in order to promote inclusion for all people, mental health service providers implement other equalities policies effectively – for example on racial equality or access for people with physical or sensory impairments;

● voluntary and statutory mental health services establish and maintain a dialogue with employers and a presence in employers' forums so that thinking on stress, best practice in human resource management and fairness at work relates to thinking on mental health. Mental health services also need to work with employers to map the gaps in the information or support available. They need to be accessible to employers, providing practical back up as well as information;

● those responsible for providing mental health services become informed on the employment schemes and structures being developed through the New Deal, as well as the specialist mental health employment services;

● ensure that the culture of low expectation in employment services for users is challenged, and provide support for users to aim for and attain work of the status they choose and feel themselves capable of;

● ensure that service users' work needs are given priority in the care management process;

● provide supported employment services so that both (prospective) employees and employers can access help to make mainstream jobs viable for more people;

● equip mental health workers (including support workers, psychiatrists, community psychiatric nurses, ASWs etc.) to support service users in gaining access to work opportunities, and to engage with employers, building it into their role. Involve users and employers in training mental health workers to be advocates and partners with respect to the world of work;

- provide support for self-employment and collective/co-operative enterprises such as social firms, so that users of mental health services have the opportunity to create jobs on terms that satisfy their needs and do not have to rely on employers only as a route to employment;

- recognise the contribution to mental health care made by support workers within the mental health system. Take steps to improve their status, for example by supporting participation in formal training and qualifications, such as the Certificate in Community Mental Health Care currently being piloted by the Mental Health Foundation.

Mental health services – education and training
The barriers between the world of education and training and mental health need to be breached at service provider level. The Panel heard much evidence of how access to education and training can be the catalyst in a return to good mental health and social inclusion.

The Panel recommends that:

- mental health service providers should build bridges with local education services, to find out what they can offer and be accessible to them. For example introduce mental health service users to the education service, or talk to teaching or administrative staff, invite staff from the education service to come and meet users and say what they offer, or advertise the mental health support service to students.

Mental health services - mental health promotion
Mental health services need to undertake public education on a twin-track approach: to promote good mental health amongst the general public, and to reduce the discrimination to which existing service users are subjected by promoting the facts about mental ill-health. The Panel recommends that:

- health authorities should support local public awareness campaigns such as those outlined in the public health White Paper (DoH 1999), and facilitate the involvement of service users from all sections of the community in such campaigns;

- mental health and primary care service providers in the statutory and voluntary sectors should work with user and advocacy organisations to promote positive understanding of mental health locally – through pro-active work with local media (rather than waiting to respond when something 'goes wrong'), links with politicians and other community leaders, and educational work with schools, employers and other community organisations.

APPENDIX A

Inquiry Panel members

Lincoln Crawford is a barrister specialising in employment and equal opportunities work.

David Crepaz-Keay is a writer on mental health issues. He is the former Chair of Survivors Speak Out, and former Vice-Chair of Wokingham Mind. He is currently Deputy Director of Mental Health Media.

Ivan Massow is Chair of Massow's (independent financial advisers), and was recently appointed Chair of the Institute of Contemporary Arts. As a result of the suicide of his partner James, he became interested in mental health issues, and works closely with the Samaritans. He also works on inclusion for the gay community, particularly in the area of insurance.

Rabbi Julia Neuberger is Chief Executive of the King's Fund, and a member of the General Medical Council. She also chaired the working party for the Sainsbury Centre for Mental Health's review of the future roles and training of mental health staff, *Pulling Together.*

Denise Platt CBE is Chief Inspector of the Social Services Inspectorate. She was previously Head of Social Services at the Local Government Association, and is a former President of the Association of Directors of Social Services. She has spent a lengthy career in social services, in both the health service and local authority.

Baroness Pola Manzila Uddin was appointed in 1998 as a working peer in the House of Lords. She has many longstanding involvements with community organisations in East London, where she trained as a social worker before going into local politics in Tower Hamlets.

APPENDIX B

Dates and venues of Panel hearings

Wednesday 9 September 1998
The King's Fund, 11–13 Cavendish Square, London

Wednesday 23 September 1998
Guildhall, Corporation of London, Gresham St, London

Thursday 1 October 1998
Cardiff International Arena, Cardiff

Thursday 26 November 1998
Guildhall, Corporation of London, Gresham St, London

APPENDIX C

Oral evidence

Peter Bates
Team Leader
Mental Health and Learning
   Disabilities
National Development Team
St Peters Court, 8 Trumpet St
Manchester M1 5LW
*(National Development Team is an
independent agency that wants new
opportunities and inclusion in
ordinary life for all people with
learning disabilities, including those
with mental health problems)*

Mike Birch
Lecturer in Broadcasting &
   Journalism Studies
Broadcasting Studies Dept
Falmouth College of Arts
Woodlane
Falmouth TR11 4RA

Samira Ben Omar
Aisling Byrne
Al-Hasaniya Moroccan Women's
   Mental Health Project
Bays 4 & 5, Trellick Tower
Golborne Road
London W10 5PL

Marilyn Bryan
(formerly) Coordinator
Awetu
Unit 5, Coopers Yard
Curran Road
Cardiff CF1 5DF
(Awetu is a black mental health project)

Jabeer Butt,
Researcher and Consultant
Race Equality Unit
Unit 27/28 Angel Gate
City Road
London EC1V 2PT

Tony Coggins
Vocational Services Manager
Lewisham & Guy's Mental Health
   Trust
Leegate House
Burnt Ash Road
Lea Green
London SE12 8RG

Sophie Corlett
Policy Director – Higher Education
National Bureau for Students with
   Disabilities (SKILL)
Chapter House
18–20 Crucifix Lane
London SE1 3JW

Alistair Cox
Coordinator
42nd Street
4th Floor, Swan Buildings
20 Swan Street
Manchester M4 5JW
*(42nd Street is a community-based
resource for young people under stress)*

Hywel Davies
Chair, Pembrokeshire Hearing
  Voices Group
c/o West Wales Action for Mental
  Health
The Tudor Rooms
Holloway
Haverfordwest
Pembrokeshire SA61 2JL

Simon Foster
Legal Director
Mind
15–19 Broadway
London E15 4BQ

Charles Fraser
Director
St Mungo's
Atlantic House
1–3 Rockley Road
London W14 ODJ
*(St Mungo's is a Registered Social
Landlord working with single homeless
people, mostly over the age of 25)*

Caroline Gooding
Information Consultant
Employers' Forum on Disability
Nutmeg House
60 Gainsford Street
London SE1 2NY

The Venerable Arthur Hawes
Archdeacon of Lincoln
Archdeacon House
Northfield Road
Quarrington
Sleaford
Lincolnshire NG34 8RT

Gail Issitt
Equal Opportunities Manager
HSBC *(formerly Midland Bank plc)*
St Magnus House
3 Lower Thames Street
London EC3R 6HA

Jo
Mental Health Service User

Lionel Joyce
Chief Executive
Newcastle NHS Trust
Westgate Road
Newcastle upon Tyne NE4 6BE

Gill Lambert
Service Standards Manager
SWALEC
Newport Road
St Mellons
Cardiff CF3 9XW
(SWALEC is a utility company)

Chrissie Lawson
(formerly) Human Resources Policy
  Manager
Tesco
Tesco House, PO Box 18
Delamare Road
Cheshunt
Herts EN8 9SL

Lorraine Lawson
Mental Health Service User

Tom Lawson
Communications Manager
Terence Higgins Trust
52–54 Grays Inn Road
London WC1X 8JU
(The Terance Higgins Trust provides
support and services for people with
HIV/AIDS, and runs sexual health
promotion campaigns)

Julian Leff
Professor of Psychiatry
Social Psychiatry Section
Institute of Psychiatry
De Crespigny Park
Denmark Hill
London SE5 8AF

Voirrey Manson
Project Manager
NHS Equality Unit
Tal-y-Garn
Pontyclun
Margannwg Ganol CF7 9XB

Micheline Mason
Alliance for Inclusive Education
Unit 2, 70 South Lambeth Road
London SW8 1RL
(The Alliance for Inclusive Education
compaigns to end compulsory
segregation in education)

Francois Matarasso
Comedia
89 Julian Road
West Bridgford
Nottingham NG2 5AL
(Comedia is an independent research
centre, which helps communities
make the most of their cultural assets)

Simon Morris
Assistant Director Community
  Services
Jewish Care
Michael Sobell Community Centre
Limes Avenue
London NW11 9DJ
(Jewish Care is Anglo-Jewry's largest
social services organisation catering
for the needs of the community living
in London and the South East)

Tom O'Brien
General Practitioner
Jubilee Medical Centre
Croxteth
Liverpool L11 4UG

Rachel Perkins
Clinical Director
Rehabilitation Services
South West London & St George's
  Mental Health NHS Trust
Springfield Hospital
61 Glenburnie Rd
London SW17 7DJ

Shafiqur Rahman
Imam
The Chaplaincy
Royal London Hospitals Trust
Whitechapel Road
London E1 1BB

Sharon Ridgeway
Research Psychologist
National Centre for Mental Health
  & Deafness
Mental Health Services of Salford
Bury New Road
Prestwich M25 3BL

Crispin Truman
Director
Toby Seddon
(formerly) Development Worker
Revolving Doors Agency
45–49 Leather Lane
London EC1N 7TJ
*(Revolving Doors Agency is an
independent charity working to
improve care for people with mental
health problems who come into
contact with the criminal justice
system. All inquiries to the Director)*

Jan Turnbull
Mental Health Access Officer
Coventry Social Services
162 Henley Road
Coventry CV2 1BW

Perry Walker
Director
New Economics Foundation
Cinammon House
6–8 Cole Street
London SE1 4YH
*(The New Economics Foundation
promotes practical and creative
approaches for a just and sustainable
economy)*

Sue Wallis
Equal Opportunities Consultant
The Boots Company
Group Headquarters
Thane Road
Nottingham NG2 3AA

APPENDIX D

Written submissions

Mind would like to thank all those who sent in written submissions. A number of respondents requested complete anonymity and are therefore not included in this Appendix. All evidence was of great value to the Inquiry, and informed the Panel's recommendations.

3I plc
91 Waterloo Rd
London SE1 8XP

Abantu
1 Winchester House
11 Cranmer Road
London SW9 6EJ

The Advocacy Project
Tina Robinson
Granby Community Mental Health
  Group
91 Upper Parliament Street
Liverpool L8 7LB

African-Caribbean Mental Health Project
Zion Community Health and Resource
  Centre
Zion Crescent
Hulme
Manchester M15 5FQ

Age Concern East Sussex
Mandy Love & Isabelle Simon-Evans
54 Cliffe High Street
Lewes, East Sussex BN7 2AN

Age Exchange
The Reminiscence Centre
11 Blackheath Village
London SE3 9LA

Alcohol Recovery Project
Choices (Alcohol Services to Black
  Communities)
Vicky Jones, Project Manager
140–2 Stockwell Road
London SW9 9TQ

Robin Allen QC
Cloisters
1 Pump Court, Temple
London EC4Y 7AA

Anglia University
Professor David Brandon
School of Social Work
East Road
Cambridge CB1 1PT

ASDA Stores
Marie Gill
Employee Relations Manager
Southbank, Great Wilson Street
Leeds LS11 5AD

Asian Women's Community
  Development Project
Manchester City Council
Corporate Performance
Room 3029, Town Hall Extension
Manchester M60 2LA

Association of Community Health
   Councils for England & Wales
Frances Presley
Earlsmead House
30 Drayton Park
London N5 1PB

Association of Educational
   Psychologists
Karen Brown
Senior Administrative Officer
26 The Avenue
Durham DH14ED

Avalon NHS Trust
Sue Hales, Day Hospital Manager
Magnolia House
56a Preston Road
Yeovil
Somerset BA20 2BN

Anne Bagnall

Bob Bancroft

Bank of England
Chris Bailey, Press Officer
Threadneedle Street
London EC2R 8AH

Bank of Scotland
David Lind, Employee Relations
Orchard Brae House
PO Box 475
30 Queensferry Road
Edinburgh EH4 2UZ

Barbara Bannister

Barclays Bank plc
Elaine Horner
Equal Opportunities Manager
Employee Relations
PO Box 256
Fleetway House
25 Farringdon Street
London EC4A 4LP

K. W. Barker

Leslie Barker

Barnet Community Health Council
Suzanne Collins
159 Ballards Lane
London N3 1LJ

Baron Court Project
Elva London, Project Worker
69 Talgarth Road
London W14

Maureen Barraclough

James Berry

Rosanna Berry

Black Orchid
Joan Field-Thorne
Unit 6, Kuumba Project
20–22 Hepburn Road
Bristol BS2 8UD

The Body Shop International plc
Monica Newton
Watersmead
Littlehampton
West Sussex BN17 6LS

Bournemouth and Poole College of
    Further Education
Alec C. Carrotte, Programme Leader
Welfare Studies
North Road
Parkstone, Poole
Dorset BH14 0LS

BP Amoco plc
Steve Heron
Senior HR Advisor
Britannic House
1 Finsbury Circus
London EC2M 7BA

Brent Advocacy Concerns
Richard Downes, Coordinator
154 Harlesden Road
London NW10 BRX

British Aerospace
David Benwell
Equal Opportunities Adviser
(W23D) Warton Aerodrome
Preston PR4 1AX

British Airports Authority plc
Julie Harris
Compensation & Benefits Executive
130 Wilton Road
London SW1V 1LQ

British Medical Association
M. J. Lowe, Deputy Secretary
Tavistock Square
London WC1H 9JP

British Psychological Society
Michael Banks, Chair SCPEO
St Andrews House
48 Princess Road East
Leicester LE1 7DR

Bromley-by-Bow Centre
Allison Trimble
Project Director
1 Bruce Road
London E3 3HN

Ellen Brown

Jacqui Brown

M. Brown

R. Brown

Jacqueline Burrows

Ian Bynoe
c/o Mind
15–19 Broadway
London E15 4BQ

Ann Bywater

Calderdale Social Services
Mental Health Services
Horsfall House
Skircote Moor Road
Halifax HX3 OHJ

Cambridgeshire Mental Welfare
    Association Ltd
Penny Smith, Coordinator
Barrere House
100 Chesterton Road
Cambridge CB4 1ER

Cancerlink
11–21 Northdown Street
London N1 9BN

Canterbury and Faversham Forum for
    Mental Health
Nick Dent, Volunteer Coordinator
9 St John's Place
Canterbury
Kent CT1 1BD

Linda Canham

Central Lincolnshire Community
    Health Council
R. Boyfield, Chairman
348 High Street
Lincoln LN5 7NB

Chelsea & Westminster Hospital
Accident & Emergency
369 Fulham Rd
London SW10

Church of England
Board of Social Responsibility
Peter Sedgwick
Church House
Great Smith Street
London SW1P 3NZ

Church of Scotland
Gail Wilson, Community Guide
Board of Social Responsibility
Morven Day Services
90 Ardbeg Avenue
Kilmarnock
East Ayrshire KA3 2AR

Citizens Advice Bureau
Beddington and Wallington
Pauline Collis, Bureau Manager
16 Stanley Park Rd
Wallington
Surrey SM6 0EU

Citizens Advice Bureau Northwich
Kathy Doeser, Advocate
48 Chester Way
Northwich
Cheshire CW9 5JA

Citizenship Foundation
Jan Newton, Chief Executive
15 St Swithin's Lane
London EC4N 8AL

Clarendon College
Kathryn James
Mental Health Support Service
Pelham Avenue, Mansfield Rd
Nottingham NG5 1AL

Paul Cleverly

Clinical Theology Association
R. C. S. Moss, Chair
St Mary's House
Church Westcote
Oxford OX7 6SF

Richard Comaish

Commission on the future of Multi-
    Ethnic Britain
H. C. Seaford, Director
133 Aldersgate Street
London EC1 4JA

Community Housing and Therapy
Bishop Creighton House
378 Lillie Road
London SW6 7PH

Michael Coombe

Simon Coombe

Eddy Gaetan Corentin

Council for Involuntary Tranquilliser
    Addiction
Pam Armstrong
Cavendish House
Brighton Road
Liverpool L22 5NG

Rhonda Cousens

Coventry Mental Health Joint
    Commissioning Group
G. M. Henman
Planning & Development Officer
Civic Centre 1 (SS13)
Coventry CV1 5RS

Daniel

Dartford and Gravesham Advocacy
    Network
Anne Jenkins, Advocate
The Almshouses
20 West Hill
Dartford
Kent DA1 2EP

D. Davison

Melphy Dean

Depression Alliance
Anne Tysall, Group Organiser
35 Westminster Bridge Road
London SE1 7JB

Disability Awareness in Action
Rachel Hurst
11 Belgrave Road
London SW1V 1RB

Paul Dodds

John Donnelly

Laura Donohue

Jacqueline Dowson

DSS Umbrella Centre
Maureen Boyd, Project Manager
111 Mount Pleasant
Liverpool L3 5TF

Fatma Durmur

East Surrey Health Authority
Carrie Morgan
Commissioning Manager
West Park Road
Horton Lane
Epsom KT19 8PH

Eastbourne and County Healthcare
Martin Corfe
Ashen Hill, The Drive
Hellingly
Hailsham BN27 4ER

Eating Disorders Association
Nicky Bryant, Chief Executive
First Floor, Wensum House
103 Prince of Wales Road
Norwich NR1 1DW

Equip
Rosemary Turner
University House
Lancaster University
Lancaster LA1 4YW

Wendy Fletcher

D. A. Ford

Paul Foster

Ted Foster

Jim Gibson

Ron Gibson

Les Gill

Glasgow Association for Mental Health
Jenny Graydon
Director
3rd Floor
Shaftesbury House
5 Waterloo St
Glasgow G2 6AY

15–23 Gadogan Street
Glasgow G2 6QQ

Margrit Goddard

Raymond Goodman

Ruth Govan

Edward Grimley

GROW Project (Give Real Opportunities
  to Women)
Neil Morriss
65 All Saints Way, Aston
Sheffield S26 2FJ

Gwynedd Council
Arwel Wyn Owen, Policy Officer
Council Offices, Shirehall St
Caernarfon
Gwynedd LL55 1SH

Halifax plc
Gill Dawson, Equal Opportunities
  Manager
Trinity Road
Halifax HX1 2RG

Mary Hancock

Paula Hansen

Hastings Association for the Pastoral
  Care of the Mentally Ill
Befriending Scheme
Lynn Jenkins, Administrator
49 Cambridge Gardens
Hastings
East Sussex TN34 1EN

Havering Users Barking and Brentwood
  (HUBB)
J. M. Gray, Community Advocate
Suite 4, Victoria Mews
121 Victoria Road
Romford
Essex RM1 2LX

Clifford Hayes

The Health Resource Centre
Pam Carter, Project Leader
45 Uxbridge Street
Burton-upon-Trent
Staffordshire
DE14 3JR

Lindy Herrington

Highgate Centre
Eva Darlow, Deputy Manager
19–37 Highgate Road
London NW5 1JY

Homebase Ltd
Ms M. E. Arins
Personnel Administrator
Moor Allerton Centre
King Lane
Leeds LS17 5NY

The Housing Corporation
Judith Hutton, Personnel Officer
Elisabeth House
16 St Peter's Square
Manchester M2 3DF

Timothy Hughes

Hyde Plus
C. Jobber
Young People Move On Co-ordinator
11 Parrock Street
Gravesend
Kent LE1 7DR

Imperial College
School of Medicine
Michael Parker
Department of General Practice
Norfolk Place
London W2 1PG

Inchcape
33 Cavendish Square,
London W1M 9HX

Innovations
Adrienne Benham
59 Stanley Road
Earlsdon
Coventry CV5 6FG

Irish Support and Advice Service
Donal Brennan
Community Care Manager
Hammersmith Irish Centre
Blacks Road, London W6 9DT

John Jackson

Ron Johnston

Karen

Michael Kelliher

Kensington and Chelsea Joint
   Homelessness Team
J. Brodie, Social Worker
84 Pembroke Road
London W8 6NX

Kensington and Chelsea Forum
Emma Dyke
Development and Support Worker
Office 1, 7 Thorpe Close
London W10 5XL

Kilburn Irish Youth Project
Karen Gittens
Kingsgate Community Centre
107 Kingsgate Rd
London NW6 2JH

The King's Fund
Janice Robinson
Director, The Community Care
   Programme
11–13 Cavendish Square
London W1M OAN

Kerry Kirkpatrick

Krishna Yoga Mandir
Pandit K. C. Krishnatreya
Founder, Chairman of Trustees
c/o 61 Churchbury Road
Enfield EN1 3HP

Peter Lawrence

Leeds Mental Health Advocacy Group
Hilary Dyter, Coordinator
Centenary House
59 North Street
Leeds LS2 8AY

Leeds University
Judith Russell, Disabilities Officer
Room 10.2b, Red Route,
Boyle Library Building
Leeds LS2 9JT

Lichfield Diocese
B. Metcalf, Projects Officer
6 Highgate Court
Lysways Street
Walsall WS1 3AD

Anselm Lionel-Rajah

Littlewoods
Surinder Sharma
Corporate Equal Opportunities Manager
Sir John Moores Building
100 Old Hall Street
Liverpool L70 1AB

Liverpool John Moores University
P. Walton, Senior Lecturer
Law and Applied Social Studies
Josephine Butler House
1 Myrtle Street
Liverpool L7 4DN

Lloyds TSB Group plc
Jo Lewis, Head of Public Affairs
71 Lombard Street
London EC3P 3BS

Ian Lomax

London Borough of Ealing Housing
    Department
Alan Hawsworth
Mental Health Manager
1st Floor, Town Hall Annexe
Ealing New Broadway
London W5 2BY

London Borough of Haringay
Dawn Cardis
Child Protection Adviser
Social Services
Duke House, Crouch Hall Road
London N8 8HE

London Borough of Hillingdon Social
    Services
David Whittingham
Senior Social Worker
South-East Locality Community
    Mental Health Team
Mead House, Hayes End Road
Hayes End
Middlesex UB4 8EW

Lothian Anti-Poverty Alliance
Bill Scott, Coordinator
Wellgate House
200 Cowgate
Edinburgh EH1 1NQ

Rose Luckman

Eddie Makinson

Stephen Raphael Manning

Marks and Spencer plc
Equal Opportunities Dept
Michael House
Baker Street
London W1A 1DN

L. Maydwell

Paul McCarthy

Roy McConnachie

Meet-a-Mum Association
Jackie Cochrane
26 Avenue Road
South Norwood
London SE25 4DX

Mental After Care Association
Sue Greaves, Scheme Organiser
Unit 26, 26 Roundlay Road
Leeds LS7 1AB

Mental Health Services of Salford
Stephen Young, Director of Service
Development
Bury New Road
Prestwich M25 3BL

Metropolitan Police Services
Commander Hugh Orde
New Scotland Yard
Broadway
London SW1H OBG

Mental Health Foundation
20/21 Cornwall Terrace
London NW1 4QL

Mid-Yorkshire Chamber of Commerce
   and Industry Ltd
Commerce House, Wakefield Road
Aspley
Huddersfield HD5 9AA

Michael

G. Mill

Veronica Milsted

Mind in Barnsley
Ian Watson, Chief Executive
156 Sheffield Road
Barnsley S70 1JH

Mind in Birmingham
D. Hanman
District Manager
17 Graham Street
Hockley B1 3JR

Mind in Corby
Ann O'Boyle, Coordinator
18 Argyll Street
Corby NN17 1RU

Mind in Hillingdon
Madeleine King, Director
Aston House, Redford Way
Uxbridge
Middx UB9 6EG

Mind in Manchester Ltd
Rowan Purdy
Information Worker
23 New Mount Street
Manchester M4 4DE

Mind in Neath
Amanda Cox
32 Victoria Gardens
Neath SA11 3BH

Mind in Pembrokeshire
Carol Castell
Rm 28, Meadow Park
Stokes Avenue
Haverfordwest
Dyfed SA61 2RB

Mind in Tower Hamlets
Daryeelka Maanka, Richard Smith
13 Whitethorn Street
London E3 4DA

Mind in West Suffolk
The Coach House
Long Brackland
Bury St. Edmunds
Suffolk IP33 1JH

Mind in Wokingham
1 Church Cottage
Church Hill
Reading RG10 0SN

Mind in Wokingham
Pam Jenkinson
Crisis House
Station House
Station Approach
Wokingham RG40 2AP

Mind in Winsford
Jill McQuaid, Secretary
Neighbourhood Centre
Cheviot Square
Winsford, Cheshire CW7 1QS

Mind in Wycombe
Bel Vaughan, Director
1–3 Priory Avenue
High Wycombe
Bucks HP13 6SQ

Mind Over Matter
John Stuckey, Community Social
  Worker
c/o SCVS
21 Lewis Road
Sutton SM1 4BR

Minority Agricultural and Rural
  Equestrian Skills (MARES)
Janetta Longhurst
12 Marston Court, Station Road
Long Marston
Herts HP23 4QD

Moray Association for Mental
  Health Co Ltd
Jean Lynch, Manager
Unit 100b, Pinefield Business Centre
Pinefield Industrial Estate
Elgin IV30 6AN

Joyce Moseley
27 Parkholme Road
London E8 3AG

Michael Murphy

NACRO
169 Clapham Road
London SW9 0PU

Nafsiyat
Lennox Thomas, Clinical Director
278 Seven Sisters Road
London N4 2HY

National Association of Citizen
  Advice Bureaux
Jason Eden
Social Policy Development Officer
136–144 City Road
London EC1V 2QN

National Deaf Services
Leo Freeman
Occupational Therapist
Old Church, 146a Bedford Hill
London SW12 9HW

National Westminster Bank
Carol Detheridge
Diversity Manager
Level 27, Drapers Gardens
12 Throgmorton Avenue
London N10 3PE

Nationwide Building Society
Jackie Tolliday
Corporate Personnel Analyst
Kings Park Road
Moulton Park
Northampton NN3 6LL

Newham Counselling Forum
Manuela Toporowska
(now closed)

Newport CBC
David Paratt
Head of Service Planning
Civic Centre
Newport NP20 4UR

Norfolk Mental Health Care NHS Trust
Fiona Cutts, Directorate General
   Manager
Mary Chapman House
Hotblack Road
Norwich NR2 4HN

North East Essex Community
   Health Council
Kate Gill, CHC Officer
34 St Botolphs Street
Colchester CO2 7EA

Northern Ireland Electricity
Myran Pollock, Manager
Equality and Services
Danesfort, 120 Malone Road
Belfast BT9 5HT

North Notts Advocacy
W. Oldfield
Advocacy Development Worker
The Dukeries, Whinneylane
Ollerton, Newark
Notts NG22 9TD

North Tyneside Community Health
   Council
Sally Young, Chief Officer
19 Albion House
Sidney Street
North Shields NE29 OED

Northern Foods plc
Phil Ward
Beverley House
St Stephens Square
Hull
E. Yorks HU1 3XG

Norwich Union
PO Box 4
Surrey St
Norwich NR1 3NG

F. O'Brien

Olabisi Olaleye Foundation
T. O. Olaleye-Oruene, Director
Suite 44, Collingwood House
99 New Cavendish Street
London W1M 7FQ

Wayne Oldfield

Vince O'Mahony

Ian Owen

OXAIDS
David Lynch, Coordinator
Gay Men's Project
43 Pembroke Street
Oxford OX1 1BP

PACE
Julienne Dickey
34 Hartham Road
London N7 9JL

Dave Palmer

Parents' Friend
Joy Dickens
c/o Voluntary Action Leeds
Stringer House
34 Lupton Street
Leeds LS10 2QW

Pearl
Andrew Jones
The Pearl Centre
Lynch Wood
Peterborough PE2 6FY

Marilyn Phillips

Pilton Outreach Project (PROP)
c/o The Stress Centre
5 West Pilton Park
Edinburgh EH4 4EL

Ted Poole

Alec Potter

The Poverty Alliance
162 Buchanan Street
Glasgow G1 2IL

Powergen plc
Westwood Park
Westwood Way
Coventry CV4 8LG

The Psychotherapy Centre
R. K. Brian
Principal
1 Wythburn Place
London W1H 5WL

Ravidassia Centre
Roj Shard
Garden City Surgery
59 Station Road
Letchworth
Herts SA6 3BJ

Redbridge Racial Equality Council
P. E. Ballantine, Chair
Methodist Church Hall
Ilford Lane
Ilford
Essex IG1 2JZ

Jane Reed

Anthony Rees

Refugee Council
Inquiry Desk
3 Bondway
London SW8 1SJ

Rhondda Cynon Taff County Borough
  Council
Mary E. Powell, Equalities Adviser
Personnel Department
The Pavilions, Clydach Vale
Tonypandy CF40 2XX

Richer Sounds
David Robinson
Managing Director
58–62 Lower Hillgate
Stockport SK1 3AL

Richmond Fellowship
Leo Sowerby
21–22 Queens Square
Leeds Rd
Huddersfield HD2 1XN

Robbs at Tynedale Park
Alemouth Road
Hexham
Northumberland NE46 3PJ

Diana Rose

G. Roughley

Royal National Institute for Deaf People
G. Loosemoore-Reppen
Policy Officer
19–23 Featherstone Street
London EC1Y 8SL

Sainsbury Centre for Mental Health
Andrew McCulloch
134–138 Borough High Street
London SE1 1LB

Sainsbury's
Kate Walker
HR Policy-Project Manager
7th Floor, Drury House
Stamford Street
London SE1 9LL

St George's Crypt
Tony Beswick, Administrator
Great George Street
Leeds LS1 3BR

Ann Samways

Scanlink
17 Britannia Street
London WC1X 9JN

Margarette Scott

Anita Sebastian

Sheffield Social Services
Clive Clarke, Service Manager
Community Health Sheffield
Mental Health Directorate
Fulwood House
Old Fulwood Road
Sheffield S10 3TH

Kay Sheldon

Shell UK
Lindsey Cordwell
c/o Shell Centre
London SE1 7NA

Shree Ram Krishna Community Centre
Niha Patel
Alfred Street
Loughborough LE11 1NG

Ian Simmons

Heather Smith

Roy Smith

South Bedfordshire Community Health
  Care Trust
Rhoda Cunningham, Staff Nurse
Leagrave Lodge
High Street
Leagrave LU4 9JU

South Glamorgan TEC
Lindsay Charles Evans
2–7 Drake Walk
Brigantine Place, Atlantic Wharf
Cardiff CF1 5AN

South West London & St George's
  Mental Health NHS Trust
Ben Davidson
Project Coordinator
User Employment Project
61 Glenburnie Road
London SW17 8DA

South Tyneside Community Health
  Council
Ian Webb, Chief Officer
3rd Floor, Edinburgh Buildings
South Shields
Tyne & Wear NE33 1HR

Southwark Council
Carol Ugbechie, Equalities Unit
East House
35 Peckham Road
London SE5 8UB

START
Bernadette Conlon
Project Manager
Mental Health Services of Salford
Pendleton House
Broughton Road
Salford M6 6LS

Stepping Stones Programme
Jeremy Braund
The Adult College
P. O. Box 603
White Cross Education Centre
Quarry Road
Lancaster LA1 3SE

R. L. Stevens

Sue Stevens

Stress in Nursing
Ian Payne & Veronica Burton
28 Littleworth Village
Wheatley OX33 ITR

L. Susswein

Keith Thornley

Charlette Thornton

TIPP Centre (Theatre in Prisons and
  Probation)
James Thompson, Director
c/o Drama Department
Manchester University
Oxford Road
Manchester M13 9PL

Torridge Special Friends
Kate Sainsbury
Hazelhurst
20 Abbotsham Road
Bideford
Devon EX39 3AH

B. Pearl Tose

Total Care Management
Grainne Currie
Carrington Business Park
Urmston M31 4QW

Heather Trenchard

K. J. Tutt

United Biscuits
Marlene Baker
Employment Policy Manager
Church Road
West Drayton
Middlesex UB7 7PR

United Kingdom Advocacy Network
Terry Simpson, Coordinator
14–18 West Bar Green
Sheffield S1 2DA

University of Hull
Jill Manthorpe and Nicky Stanley
Dept of Social Work
Hull HU6 7RX

University of Leeds
P. Morrall
School of Healthcare Studies
The Infirmary
Great George Street, Leeds LS1 3EX

US, All Wales Survivor Network
Steve Craine
Office Suite 3
1 North Parade
Aberystwyth SY23 2JH

User Involvement Project
Laura Able
176d Uxbridge Road
London W7 3TB

The Valleys Race Equality Council
Helen Whiting, Outreach Coordinator
PACE Building
Tyfica Road
Pontypridd CF37 2DE

Graham Vest

Victory Centre
Tony Kuhl, Manager
52 Magdalen Road
Exeter EX2 4TL

M. Wadeson

Jez Ward

Robin Waterman

Sylvia Waters

West Lancs NHS Trust
Kevin Wright
Clinical Development Nurse
Ormskirk General Hospital
Wigan Road
Ormskirk L39 2AZ

M. D. Whewell

Louise Whittle

Wiltshire Racial Equality Council
Mayur Bhatt
Development Worker
Bridge House, Stallard Street
Trowbridge BA14 9AE

Women and Mental Health
Julie McNamara
15 Woodbury Street
London SW17 9RP

Women Together
Barbara Maskens
112 Elmhurst Drive
Hornchurch
Essex RM11 1PF

Workability Eastbourne
110 South Street
Eastbourne
BN21 4LZ

Judy Wurr
Consultancy and Training for
    Community Care
26 Roe Lane
Roe Green Village
London NW9 9BJ

Michael Zappara

APPENDIX E

Useful organisations

Listed below are some key organisations referred to in the report, plus other useful bodies in the mental health and social inclusion fields.

Asian Women's Textile Group
Rachel Hunter Rowe
Aston Hall
Trinity Road
Birmingham B6 6JD

Bromley-by-Bow Centre
1 Bruce Road
London E3 3HA

Bradford Home Treatment Service
Dr Pat Bracken
Edmund Street Clinic
Edmund Street
Bradford BD5 OBJ

The Capital Project
Andrea Linnell
Development Officer
West Sussex Social Services
County Hall, Tower St
Chichester
West Sussex PO19 1QT

Carers National Association
20/25 Glasshouse Yard
London EC1A 4JT

Cardboard Citizens
Adrian Jackson
146 Mare Street
London E8 3SG

'Changing Minds' Campaign
Campaign Administrator
Royal College of Psychiatrists
17 Belgrave Square
London SW1X 8PG

The Community, Safety and Partnership
    Policy Unit
The Metropolitan Police
New Scotland Yard
Broadway
London SW1H OBG

Drayton Park
Shirley McNicholas, Manager
32 Drayton Park
London N5 1PB

First Stage Access Course
Stoke Park School Community College
Dane Road
Coventry CV2 4JW

Health Education Authority/Health
    Development Agency
Trevelyan House
30 Great Peter Street
London SW1P 2HW

Joseph Rowntree Foundation
The Homestead
40 Water End
York Y030 6WP

Julian Housing Support
Tom Wilson, General Manager
1a Oak Street
Norwich NR3 3AE

The King's Fund
11–13 Cavendish Square
London W1M OAM

Looking Well Centre
Mary Robson
Pioneer Projects
32–34 Main Street
High Bertham, Lancs LA2 7HN

Manic Depression Fellowship
  (England)
8–10 High Street
Kingston upon Thames
Surrey KT1 1EY

Manic Depression Fellowship (Wales)
Barbara Parnell
1 Palmyra Place
Newport
Wales NP20 4EJ

Mediawatch,
c/o Press Office
Mind
15–19 Broadway
London E15 4BQ

Mental After Care Association
25 Bedford Square
London WC1H 3HW

Mental Health Media
London Voluntary Sector Resources
  Centre
356 Holloway Road
London N7 6PA

Merton Education Authority
Integrated Support Services (ISS)
Lesley Kaufman
The Canterbury Centre
Canterbury Road
Morden
Surrey SM4 6PT

National Association for Care and
  Resettlement of Offenders
169 Clapham Road
London SW9 OPU

NHS Executive London
40 Eastbourne Terrace
London W2 3QR

National Schizophrenia Fellowship
30 Tabernacle Street
London EC2A 4DD

Richmond Fellowship
8 Addison Road
London W14 8DJ

Sandwell College
Tracey Austin, Section Leader
Mental Health Provision
High Street
West Bromwich
West Midlands B70 8DW

Sound Sense
The Voice of Community Music
Riverside House
Rattlesden
Bury St Edmunds IP30 0SF

Stockport Healthcare NHS Trust
Ash House
Poplar Grove
Stockport SK2 7JD

Stockport Mind
Terry Biddington
Dove House
65 Union Street
Stockport SK1 3NP

Theatr Fforwm Cymru
Goodwick Community Centre
New Hill
Goodwick
Pembrokeshire SA64 ODH

TIPP (Theatre in Prisons and
    Probation Centres)
c/o Drama Department
University of Manchester
Oxford Road
Manchester M13 9PL

Turning Point
New Loom House
101 Back Church Lane
London E1 1LU

REFERENCES AND BIBLIOGRAPHY

Amado, A. N. (ed.) (1993) *Friendships and Community Connections between People with and without Developmental Disabilities* (Baltimore: Paul H. Brookes)

Angus, J. & Murray, F. (1996) *Evaluation Frameworks, Criteria and Methods in Art for Health* (London: King's Fund)

Audit Commission (1994) *Finding a Place: A Review of Mental Health* (London: The Stationery Office)

Austin, T. (1999) 'Exploring mental health at Sandwell College' *A Life in the Day* 3, 1

Aveneri, S. & de Shalit, A. (1992) *Communitarianism and Individualism* (Oxford: Oxford University Press)

Baron, R. C. *et al.* (1996) *Strengthening the Work Incentive Provisions of the Social Security Act to Encourage Persons with Serious Mental Illness to Work at their Potential* (Washington DC: Social Security Administration)

Barrow, G. (1998) *Disaffection and Inclusion: A Mainstream Approach to Difficult Behaviour* (Bristol: CSIE)

Bates, P. (1996) 'Stuff as dreams are made of' *Health Services Journal* 33, 4 April.

Beard, M. L. (1992) 'Social networks' *Psychosocial Rehabilitation Journal* 16, 2

Becker, S. & Silburn, R. (1999) *We're in this Together: Conversations with Families in Caring Relationships* (London: Carers National Association)

Bell, D. (ed.) (1993) *Communitarianism and its Critics* (Oxford: Clarendon Press)

Beresford, P. & Turner, M. (1997) *It's Our Welfare: Report of the Citizen's Commission on the Future of the Welfare State* (London: National Institute for Social Work)

Bond, G. R., Drake, R. E., Mueser, K. T. & Becker, D. R. (1997) 'An update on supported employment for people with severe mental illness' *Psychiatric Services* 48, 3

Bracken, P. & Thomas, P. (1999) 'Home treatment in Bradford' *OpenMind* 95, Jan/Feb

Brugha, T. S. (1991) 'Support and personal relationships' in Bennet, D. H. & Hugh, L. (eds) *Community Psychiatry: The Principles* (Edinburgh: Churchill Livingstone)

Bynoe, I. (1998) 'Community, rights and responsibilities: ethical issues' *Mind Inquiry Panel Briefing* 4 (London: Mind)

Callanan, M. M., Dunne, T. P., Morris, D. P. & Stem, R. D. (1997) *Primary Care, Serious Mental Illness and the Local Community: Developing a Commissioning Framework* (Kent: Salomons Centre)

Carr, E. G. & Carlson, J. I. (1993) 'Reduction of severe behaviour problems in the community using a multi-component treatment approach' *Journal of Applied Behaviour Analysis* 26, 2

Centre for Studies on Inclusive Education (1996) *The Integration Charter* (Bristol: CSIE)

Clements, L. (1998) 'Act of weakness' *Community Care* 8–14 January

Clough, P. & Lindsay, G. (1991) *Integration and the Support Service: Changing Roles in Special Education* (London: NFER-Nelson)

Commission for Racial Equality (1998*) Racial Equality Means Business: Case Studies 1996-8* (London: CRE)

Craven, M. (1995) *The International Covenant on Economic, Social and Cultural Rights* (Oxford: Clarendon Press)

Croall, J. (1997) *LETS Act Locally* (London: Gulbenkian Foundation)

Department of Health (1993) *Legal Powers on the Care of Mentally Ill People in the Community: Report of the Internal Review* (London: DoH)

Department of Health (1994) *The Health of the Nation Key Area Handbook: Mental Illness* (London: The Stationery Office)

Department of Health (1998) *Our Healthier Nation* (London: The Stationery Office)

Department of Health (1999) *Saving Lives: Our Healthier Nation* (London: The Stationery Office)

Department of Health (1999) *National Service Framework for Mental Health: Modern Standards and Service Models* (London: DoH) (www.doh.gov.uk/nsf/mentalhealth)

Evans, G., Felce, D., De Paiva, S. & Todd, S. (1992) 'Observing the delivery of a domiciliary support service' *Disability, Handicap and Society* 7, 1

Felce, D. (1988) 'Evaluating the extent of community integration following the provision of staffed residential alternatives to institutional care' *Irish Journal of Psychology* 9, 2

Fernando, S., Ndegwa, D. & Wilson, M. (1998) *Forensic Psychiatry, Race and Culture* (London: Routledge)

Firth, H. & Rapley, M. (1989) *Making Acquaintance* (Northumberland: Northumberland Health Authority District Psychology Service)

Foster, A. & Roberts, V. Z. (eds) (1999) *Managing Mental Health in the Community: Chaos and Containment* (London: Routledge)

Friedli, L. (1999) 'From the margins to the mainstream: the public health potential of mental health promotion' (unpublished) (London: Health Education Authority)

Friedli, L. & Scherzer, A. (1996) *Positive Steps: Mental Health and Young People – Attitudes and Awareness among 11–14 Year Olds* (London: Health Education Authority)

Further Education Funding Council (1996) *Inclusive Learning – Principles and Recommendations: A Summary of the Findings of the Learning Difficulties and/or Disabilities Committee* (The Tomlinson Report) (Coventry: FEFC)

Gilbert, T. (1993) 'A systematic approach to care' in Bridgen, P. & Todd, M. (eds) *Concepts in Community Care for People with a Learning Difficulty* (Basingstoke: Macmillan)

Glozier, N. (1998) 'The workplace effects of the stigmatisation of depression' *Journal of Occupational and Environmental Medicine* 40, 783–800

Glozier, N. (1999) 'Disability Discrimination Act 1995 and mental illness' *Psychiatric Bulletin* 23, 3-6

Grove, B. (1998) 'Making New Deal a good deal for mental health' *Centre for Mental Health Services Development Conference Report* (London: CMHSD)

Grove, B. Freudenberg, M., Harding, A. & O'Flynn, D. (1997) *The Social Firm Handbook* (Brighton: Pavilion)

Hart, L. (1999) 'The reliable kettle' *OpenMind* 96, March/April

Hoggett, P., Razzaque, K., & Barker, I. (1999) *Urban Regeneration and Mental Health* (London: King's Fund)

Home Office (1993) 'Electoral registration of mentally ill or learning disabled (mentally handicapped) people: Code of Practice Note no. 5, 27 August' *Circular RPA 379* (London: Home Office)

Home Office (1997) *Rights Brought Home* (London: The Stationery Office)

Home Office (1998) *Speaking up for Justice: Report of the Interdepartmental Working Group on the Treatment of Vulnerable or Intimidated Witnesses in the Criminal Justice System* (London: Home Office)

Howarth, C., Kenway, P., Palmer, G. & Street, C. (1998) *Monitoring Poverty and Social Exclusion: Labour's Inheritance* (York: Joseph Rowntree Foundation)

Kind, P., Dolan, P., Gudex, C. & Williams, A. (1998) 'Variations in population health status: results from a UK national questionnaire study' *British Medical Journal* 316, 736–41

Leach, J. (1996) 'Integrating students with mental health problems into community education' (unpublished) (Oxford: Restore, Manzil Way, Cowley Rd, Oxford OX4 1YH)

Lindow, V. & Morris, J. (1993) *User Participation in Community Care Services* (Leeds: Community Care Support Force)

Lindow, V. (1996) *User Involvment: Community Service Users as Consultants and Trainers* (London: Department of Health)

Link, B. G., Rahav, M., Phelan, J. C. & Nuttbrock , L. (1997) ' On stigma and its consequences: evidence from a longitudinal study of men with dual diagnosis of mental illness and substance abuse' *Journal of Health and Social Behaviour* 38, 177–90

Lord, J. & Pedlar, A. (1991) 'Life in the community: four years after the closure of an institution' *Mental Retardation* 29, 4

Ludlum, C. D. (1993) *Tending the Candle: A Booklet for Circle Facilitators* (Manchester CT: Communitas Inc.)

Lutfiyya, Z. M. (1991) *Tony Santi and the Bakery: The Roles of Facilitation, Accommodation and Interpretation* (Syracuse: Syracuse University Center on Human Policy)

MacArthur Foundation (1999) *Violence Risk Assessment Study* (Charlottesville, Va: MacArthur Foundation) (http://neds.sys.virginia.edu/macarthur)

MacIntyre, A. (1980) *After Virtue* (London: Duckworth)

Mancuso, L. (1993) *Case Studies on Reasonable Accommodations for Workers with Psychiatric Disabilities* (Washington DC: Washington Business Group on Health)

Manning, C. & White, P. (1995) 'Attitudes of employers to the mentally ill' *Psychiatric Bulletin* 19, 541–3

Mental Health Foundation (1994) *Creating Community Care: Report of the Mental Health Foundation Inquiry into Community Care for People with Severe Mental Illness* (London: Mental Health Foundation)

Mental Health Foundation (1999) *The Big Picture: Promoting Children and Young People's Mental Health* (London: Mental Health Foundation)

Mental Health Foundation (1999) *CrisisPoint* (London: MHF)

Miller, C. & King, E. (1999) 'Managing for social cohesion' (London: Office for Public Management)

Mind (1997) *Older People and Mental Health* (London: Mind Policy Unit)

Mind (1998) *The Bird and the Word* (London: Mind)

Mind/HEA (1998) 'Why use labels when they don't fit?' *Postcard Series* (London: Mind/HEA)

Mind (1998) *International Examples of Projects Aiming to Combat Stigma/Discrimination Towards People with Mental Health Problems* (London: Mind Information Unit)

Moore, C. & Gawith, L. (1998) *Missed Opportunities* (London: Sainsbury Centre for Mental Health)

Moore, C. & McCulloch, A. (1998) *Acute Problems* (London: Sainsbury Centre for Mental Health)

Mullen, P., Wallace, C., Burgess, P., Palmer, S., Ruschena, D. & Browne, C. (1998) 'Serious criminal offending and mental disorder: case linkage study' *British Journal of Psychiatry* 172, 485–90

Murphy, E. (1991) *After the Asylums* (London: Faber & Faber)

National Association for the Care and Resettlement of Offenders (1999) *Children, Health and Crime: A Report by NACRO's Committee on Children and Crime* (London: NACRO)

National Association for the Care and Resettlement of Offenders (1999) *Reducing Conflict, Building Communities: The Role of Mediation in Tackling Crime and Disorder* (London: NACRO)

Office for National Statistics (1996) 'Physical complaints, service use and treatment of residents with psychiatric disorders' *OPCS Surveys of Psychiatric Morbidity in Great Britain,* Report 5 (London: The Stationery Office)

Office for National Statistics (1998) *Labour Force Survey* (London: The Stationery Office)

Palmer, A. (1993) 'Less equal than others: a survey of lesbians and gay men at work' *Stonewall Survey* (London: Stonewall)

Parker, M. (1998) 'Individualism' in Chadwick R. & Levitt M. (eds) M. *Ethical Issues in Community Health Care* (London: Arnold)

Parker, M. (ed.) (1998) *Ethics and Community in the Health Care Professions* (London: Routledge)

Patrick, H. (1994) *There's No Law Against It!* (Glasgow: Scottish Association for Mental Health)

Pearpoint, J., O'Brien, J. & Forest, M. *The PATH Workbook* (Inclusion Press)

Pedler, M. (1998) 'Mind's response to *Speaking up for Justice: Report of the Interdepartmental Working Group in the Treatment of Vulnerable or Intimidated Witnesses in the Criminal Justice System'* (London: Mind Policy Unit)

Perkins, R., Buckfield, R. & Choy, D. (1997) 'Access to employment: a supported employment project to enable mental health service users to obtain jobs within mental health teams' *Journal of Mental Health* 6, 3

Perkins, R. & Repper, J. (1996) *Working Alongside People with Mental Health Problems* (London: Chapman & Hall)

Philo, G. (1996) *Media and Mental Distress* (London: Addison Wesley Longman)

Poverty Alliance (1998) *Social Inclusion in Scotland: A Framework for Development* (Glasgow: Poverty Alliance)

Read, J. & Baker, S. (1996) *Not Just Sticks and Stones: A Survey of the Discrimination Experienced by People with Mental Health Problems* (London: Mind)

Repper, J. & Brooker, C. (1996) *A Review of Public Attitudes Towards Mental Health Facilities in the Community* (Sheffield: University of Sheffield Centre for Health & Related Research)

Repper, J., Sayce, L., Strong, S., Willmot, J. & Haines, M. (1997) *Tall Stories from the Back Yard: A Survey of Nimby Opposition to Community Mental Health Facilities Experienced by Key Service Providers in England and Wales* (London: Mind)

Richardson, A. & Ritchie, J. (1989) *Developing Friendships: Enabling People with Learning Difficulties to Make and Maintain Friends* (London: PSI/SCPR)

Rickford, F. (1997) 'Bad press: mental health groups target young people' *Community Care* 28 August–3 Sept

Rogers, A., Pilgrim, D. & Lacey, R. (1993) *Experiencing Psychiatry* (London: Macmillan)

Royal College of Psychiatrists (1998) *Changing Minds: Every Family in the Land: Recommendations for the Implementation of a 5-year Strategy* 1998–2003 (London: Royal College of Psychiatrists)

Sainsbury Centre for Mental Health (1998) *Keys to Engagement: Review of Care for People with Severe Mental Illness who are Hard to Engage with Services* (London: Sainsbury Centre for Mental Health)

Sandel, M. (1981) *Liberalism and the Limits of Justice* (Cambridge: Cambridge University Press)

Saxby, H., Thomas, M., Felce, D. & De Kock, U. (1986) 'The use of shops, cafes and public houses by severely and profoundly mentally handicapped adults' *British Journal of Mental Subnormality* 32

Sayce, L. (1992) *Eve Fights Back* (London: Mind)

Sayce, L. (1997) 'Stigma and social exclusion: top priorities for mental health policies' *Eurohealth* 3, 3

Sayce, L. (1998) 'Stigma, discrimination and social exclusion: what's in a word?' *Journal of Mental Health* 7, 4

Sayce, L. & Measey, L. (1999) 'Strategies to reduce social exclusion for people with mental health problems' *Psychiatric Bulletin* 23

Sayce, L. & Morris, D. (1998) 'Outsiders coming in? Achieving social inclusion for people with mental health problems' unpublished (London: Mind)

Sayce, L. & Willmot, J. (1997) *Gaining Respect: Preventing and Tackling Community Opposition to Mental Health Facilities* (London: Mind)

Schalock, R. L. & Lilley, M. A. (1986) 'Placement from community based mental retardation programmes: how well do clients do after 8–10 years?' *American Journal of Mental Deficiency* 90, 6

Sheldon, K. (1999) 'Stringing the net together' *OpenMind* 96, March/April

Sinclair, L. (1986) 'Practices of employers towards people with a mental disorder' (unpublished report for Mind), cited in Rogers *et al.* (1993) op. cit.

Social Exclusion Unit (1998) *Truancy and School Exclusion Report* (London: The Stationery Office)

Social Exclusion Unit (1999) 'What's it all about?' *Cabinet Office Website* (www.cabinet-office.gov.uk/seu/index/faqs.html)

Stein, L. I., Diamond, R. J. & Factor, R. M. (1990) 'A system approach to the care of persons with schizophrenia' in Herz, M. I., Keith, S. T. & Docherty, J. P. (eds) (1990) *Handbook of Schizophrenia 4: Psychosocial Treatment of Schizophrenia* (Oxford: Elsevier)

Street, C. (1999) 'Monitoring poverty and social exclusion among children and young adults' *Young Minds* 38, Jan/Feb

Sulek, J. (1999) 'The Disability Discrimination Act 1995: the case of Goodwin v. the Patent Office' *OpenMind* 95, Jan/Feb 1999

Taylor, P. J. & Gunn, J. (1999) 'Homicides by people with mental illness: myth and reality' *British Journal of Psychiatry* 174, 9–14

Tilford, S., Delaney, F. & Vogels, M. (1997) *Effectiveness of Mental Health Promotion Interventions: A Review* (London: HEA)

UNESCO (1994) *World Conference on Special Needs Education*, Salamanca (Geneva: UNESCO)

Wells, K. 'Out-of-hours help' (1999) *OpenMind* 96, March/April

Welsh, Knox & Brett (1994) 'Acting positively: positive action under the Race Relations Act 1976' *Department of Employment Research Series* 36 (London: Department of Employment)

Welsh Office (1999) *Building an Inclusive Wales: Tackling the Social Exclusion Agenda* (Cardiff: Welsh Office)

Wilkinson, R. G. *Unhealthy Societies: The Afflictions of Inequality* (London: Routledge 1996)

Wilson, M. & Francis, J. (1997) *Raised Voices: African-Caribbean and African Mental Health Service Users' Views and Experiences* (London: Mind)

Winn-Owen, J. (1998) *The Role of the Humanities in Medicine, Arts and Wellbeing: Beyond the Millennium* (Oxford: Nuffield Trust)

Wolff, G., Pathare, S., Craig, T. & Leff, J. (1996) 'Public education for community care' *British Journal of Psychiatry* 168

Wollheim, B. (1996) *Culture Makes Communities* (York: Joseph Rowntree Foundation)

Women Against Rape & Legal Action for Women (1995) *Dossier: The Crown Prosecution Service and the Crime of Rape* (London: WAR/LAW)

GLOSSARY

antipsychotic – a form of drug used in the treatment of psychosis. Antipsychotics were previously known as neuroleptics (see below), and both terms are still in use.

Disability Discrimination Act (DDA) 1995 – legislation that makes it unlawful to discriminate against disabled persons in connection with employment and the provision of goods, facilities and services.

dual diagnosis – a term used to refer to co-existing mental health problems and substance misuse problems, or to co-existing mental health problems and learning difficulties.

electroconvulsive therapy (ECT) – a form of treatment for depression and some other conditions in which an electric current is passed across the brain, in order to induce an epileptic fit. 'Modified ECT' is performed under general anaesthetic and with the use of a muscle relaxant.

hajib – a headcovering worn by Muslim women.

Health Action Zones – part of the Labour Government's targeting of areas of England with particularly high levels of ill-health. HAZs aim to bring together public, private and voluntary organisations to reshape local health and social services, and to improve the health of their local populations. There are currently 26 zones, with lifespans of between of 5 and 10 years.

Health Education Authority (HEA)/Health Development Agency (HDA) – the Health Education Authority is a Government body charged with promoting public health. The Government's 1999 White Paper *Saving Lives: Our Healthier Nation* announced the restructuring of the HEA, to be renamed the Health Development Agency from January 2000. The new HDA's remit is to ensure that health organisations and practitioners base their work on the highest standards, by, amongst other things, maintaining an up-to-date map of the evidence base for public health and health improvement.

Health of the Nation targets – established by the then Conservative Government in the 1992 White Paper *The Health of the Nation*, which outlined a health strategy for England. Mental health was chosen as one of five key areas, and targets for improvement included reducing suicide and improving 'social functioning' by the year 2000. In February 1998 the current Labour Government produced the Green Paper *Our Healthier Nation*, which set out plans for improving health and reducing health inequalities. These plans were finalised in the 1999 White Paper *Saving Lives: Our Healthier Nation*, which confirmed mental illness as one of the four key areas for improvement, and set a target of reducing suicide by at least one-fifth by 2010.

Healthy Living Centres – a Lottery-funded initiative to tackle root causes of ill health, targeting deprived people and areas. HLCs aim to improve the quality of life of local people through projects that take a holistic approach to health and complement existing programmes. Examples include exercise schemes, food co-operatives, arts work in GP surgeries, and development of LETS schemes (see below).

local exchange trading systems (LETS) – local cashless trading schemes. Members trade goods and services with each other – anything from haircuts to music lessons, therapies, ironing or DIY – using a form of 'currency' specific to the scheme. A way of accessing services and goods without money, and valuing people's skills and time outside paid employment.

Mental Health Act (MHA) (1983) – legislation setting out the circumstances in which a person defined as mentally disordered can be compulsorily detained and treated in hospital ('sectioned'). It also provides safeguards such as Mental Health Review Tribunals, and second opinions for certain treatments.

National Service Framework for Mental Health – published in September 1999, it sets out the Government's guidance on the level and balance of mental health services needed in each locality in England for adults of working age. It contains within its seven key 'standards' explicit reference to the need to promote social inclusion for mental health service users.

neuroleptic – a form of drug used in the treatment of psychosis. Can cause tardive dyskinesia (see below). The term neuroleptic is now generally being replaced by 'antipsychotic' (see above).

New Deal – a variety of Government programmes and schemes providing employment advice, work and training opportunities, in particular for young adults, lone parents, people with disabilities or long-term health problems and other unemployed people and their partners. It forms part of the

Government's welfare to work (see below) strategy.

ONE – a new 'gateway' to the welfare benefits system that is being piloted in twelve areas from 1999. ONE provides work-focused advice for people claiming benefits, as well as information on benefits and a single point of contact with the system. It aims to provide a more individualised service. Meetings with a personal adviser become a compulsory part of the claims process for people in the pilot areas from April 2000.

Public Health Observatories – announced in the 1999 White Paper *Saving Lives: Our Healthier Nation*, PHOs will be established in every NHS region, and will monitor local health and disease trends and address gaps in health information.

social capital – the combined qualities of tolerance, reciprocity and civic engagement and association within communities; the strength of the social fabric of a community. Researchers, notably Richard Wilkinson (1996), have pointed to the link between social capital and mortality rates.

Social Exclusion Unit (SEU) – set up by the new Labour Government in 1997, the SEU reports directly to the Prime Minister. The SEU's aim is to 'improve understanding of social exclusion, to promote co-operation between Government Departments, and to make recommendations to tackle social exclusion more effectively, in particular to shift the focus of policies towards prevention rather than merely dealing with the consequences of social exclusion' (SEU 1999).

social firms – small businesses that employ a significant proportion of disabled people in their workforce. They provide a supportive work environment within a commercial enterprise. The aim is to provide real jobs for real pay and offer customers high-quality products or services.

Sure Start – a Government initiative funding locally-based projects that will integrate and extend services for families and children under the age of 4 who live in areas of disadvantage. Aims to work with parents to ensure that their children are healthy, confident and ready to thrive when they start school.

tardive dyskinesia – a movement disorder, characterised by involuntary movements such as lip-smacking, grimacing, and writhing of the limbs. Most commonly caused as a (sometimes permanent) side-effect of antipsychotics (see above).

welfare to work – the Government's strategy for promoting employment and independence, and reducing expenditure on social security, with the objective 'work for those who can and security for those who cannot'. It includes changes to some benefits and the system for claiming them (see ONE above), the introduction of tax credits for working families and disabled people, and various New Deal (see above) programmes for groups disadvantaged in the labour market.

whole system events – events that gather a whole organisation or collection of interested parties in one place and enable them to talk about issues affecting them as a whole. Communication changes dramatically, and people have a sense of the whole and a voice in the process of change.

INDEX

Sayce, Liz 32
schizophrenia, diagnosis of 10, 14, 15, 16
Schizophrenia Media Agency 74
Seddon, Toby 39, 106, 143
Shafiqur Rahman 27, 142
social capital 64, 116, 175
social exclusion *see* exclusion, social
Social Exclusion Unit xiv, 1, 4, 118, 175
social firms xiv, 52-3, 121, 126, 136, 175
social inclusion *see* inclusion, social
Somalia, people of 27
South Bedfordshire Community Health Care Trust 101
South Tyneside Community Health Council 36
South West London and St George's Mental Health NHS Trust 68, 100, 135
special needs 69
specialist services ix, 38-9
spirituality 24
Stamp Out Stigma 93
Stanley, Nicky 18, 88-9, 91
Stockport Health Care NHS Trust 77
suicide 10, 57
Sure Start 175

tardive dyskinesia 30, 46, 175
Theatr Fforwm Cymru 72
Theatre in Prisons and Probation Centres (TIPP) 94, 95
therapeutic earnings 15
Turnbull, Jan 18, 19, 90, 103, 143

Uddin, Pola Manzila vi, 138

unemployment, amongst users of mental health services x, 6-8, 11-17, 41-8
users, of mental health services
attitudes towards 23, 27-8, 31, 49, 50-1, 110-11
autonomy of 53-6
effects of medication on 30-1
in education 17-20, 42-3, 46, 109-10, 122-3, 129-30
in employment 6-7, 11-17, 50-3, 65-9, 80-86, 108-9, 115, 120-22, 126-7
exclusion of x-xii, 6-45, 48-65, 118-9
inclusion of xii-xvi, 65-9, 69-72, 72-4, 80-6, 86-91, 91-6, 99-107, 114-7, 118-9, 133
and jury service 59, 125
minority ethnic 10, 12, 27, 32-3, 34
ostracisation of xi, 27-8, 31, 110-11
social networks 27-8, 31, 110-11
voting rights 59, 125
young 36-9, 42, 44, 69-71, 106-8, 113, 134

value, of a person ix, 14, 41-2, 51-3, 62, 97, 111
violence, link with mental ill-health xv, 8-9, 56-9, 63 *see also* crime; homicide
users as victims of 8, 10
voting rights 59, 125

Walker, Perry 52, 61, 95, 143
Wallis, Sue 16, 143

welfare to work 14-5, 67, 176 *see also* New Deal; ONE
whole system events 61, 176
witnesses, selection 3
Wurr, Judy 101

young users of mental health services 36-9, 42, 44, 69-71, 106-8, 113, 134

Cognitive-Behavioural Ther

Cognitive-behavioural therapy (CBT) has been extensively researched and shown to be solidly underpinned by evidence. Broadly applicable across a wide range of personal and social problems – from depression and phobias to child behavioural problems – it is only now beginning to be used to its full potential in health and social care practice.

This second edition of *Cognitive-Behavioural Therapy* is comprehensively revised and updated. It takes into account the significant amount of new research in the discipline, and integrates theory, research and practice. The text includes plentiful case studies from across health and social care to illustr   erent professional circumstances. Top

DATE

- ☐ a discussion of   velopment and distinctive features of CBT;
- ☐ a comprehensive review of research on learning and cognition, examining the therapeutic implications of these studies;
- ☐ a thorough guide to assessment and therapeutic procedures, including methods of evaluation;
- ☐ illustrations of the main methods of helping with case examples from social work, nursing and psychotherapy;
- ☐ consideration of the ethical implications of such methods as part of mainstream practice.

Cognitive-Behavioural Therapy is written in a lively and accessible style, and is designed to give a thorough grounding in cognitive-behavioural methods and their application. It is essential reading for students and professionals in psychology, social work, psychiatric nursing and psychotherapy.

Brian Sheldon is Emeritus Professor of Applied Social Research at the University of Exeter, UK. A registered Cognitive Behavioural Therapist, he is also a qualified psychiatric nurse, a qualified social worker and holds a PhD in psychology. He was previously Director of the Centre for Evidence-Based Social Services in the medical school at the University of Exeter.